BIG LITTLE LEGENDS

BIG LITTLE LEGENDS

How Everyday Leaders Build Irresistible Brands

GAIR MAXWELL

Foreword by Robert Rose

**PAGE
TWO**

Cataloguing in publication information is available from Library and Archives Canada.
ISBN 978-1-77458-166-7 (paperback)
ISBN 978-1-77458-167-4 (ebook)

Page Two
pagetwo.com

Edited by Melissa Edwards
Proofread by Alison Strobel
Cover and interior design by Jennifer Lum
Cover concept by Dana Zilic
Cover illustrations by Gillian Newland and Jeffrey Winocur
Interior illustrations by Jeffrey Winocur
Printed in Canada

biglittlelegends.com

This book is dedicated to the memory of my mother,
who insisted "there is no such word as can't,"
the legacy of my father, who went out and proved it,
and the many gifts from Dana,
who inspired me to believe it.

CONTENTS

Part III: Medium + Message

Part IV: Bigger Than Your Backyard

FOREWORD
The Wizard of Pause

HUSTLE. BE REMARKABLE; be special. Obsess or be average. Differentiate.

Every day we are urged, and urge others, to do something different than we did the day before. Breathless book titles, blog headlines and motivational speakers alike all tell us that in order to succeed, we need to figure out how to create uniquely emotional, intelligent or courageous things. There's no time to take a knee, to take a pause. We need to do it every... single... day.

It's exhausting.

Is it any wonder then that by the time Dorothy and her three friends, Scarecrow, Cowardly Lion and Tin Man discover that the Wizard of Oz is simply an ordinary man, and a "very bad wizard," they are not only disappointed, but they are also angry? "What about the heart that you promised the Tin Man, and the courage that you promised Cowardly Lion?" demands the Scarecrow.

It's at that moment that the Wizard does something extraordinary. He grants each of their wishes. But he pauses for each one with a special brand of magic: a story. He tells each that where he comes from, the extraordinary is always found in what seems unremarkable at the time.

He finishes each of the three stories by saying, "but, they have one thing you haven't got." He then gives each of them something that, at first, seems unremarkable. But each gift enables them to take a moment to find remarkable opportunity within their own true origin story.

The Scarecrow earns his diploma. The Cowardly Lion receives a medal of honor. The Tin Man gets his testimonial. But the real gift is the illumination of an origin story that each now recognizes as the source of their own remarkable capabilities.

By definition, no one can be remarkable every single day. If you were, the sheer uniformity of your remarkableness would make it unremarkable. Likewise, you can't exponentially outhustle yourself more tomorrow than you hustled today. If you hustled only one hour on Monday, and then doubled your hustle every day thereafter, you'd be out of hustle hours by Friday.

Did I mention it's exhausting?

But, what if there did exist some magical way that you could bottle what the Wizard gave to the Scarecrow, the Cowardly Lion and the Tin Man?

Can you bottle the opportunity for remarkable intelligence? Heart? Courage?

You can. You're experiencing it right now.

In the book that follows this foreword, you will learn how some of today's most visionary brands started out with opportunities no different than yours. The moment of truth of their incredible journeys began with what seemed, at the time, to be the most unremarkable of pauses: the moment of reflection that comes just after the click of a button, the theft of something unmissed, an average radio advertisement, a phone call or even a round of golf.

It may seem as if you're holding just another book about marketing. But whether it is, or not, is your choice. The secret of becoming extraordinary is that you access those opportunities through the quiet ordinariness of the pauses that follow what (at the time) seem to be the mundane events of life.

They can be the moments that change everything.

What Gair Maxwell has created with this book is nothing short of wizardry. He has not done anything that you couldn't do—but he has something you haven't got. Yet.

The stories.

Gair has carefully, thoughtfully and purposely pinpointed the exact moments in time—the pauses—that cue the storyteller to smile and say, "and the rest, as they say, is history."

The stories you're about to read are your diploma, your medal, your testimonial. They will open your universe to the possibilities that only you can create: the origin story of your own remarkable future.

You're about to discover yourself in the stories that follow. You'll see yourself in the pauses that lie between ordinary events, and the extraordinary achievements that follow. And the best part is that they are almost always found in the interactions you have with the people, places and events that are closest to you.

Let's not forget that in *The Wizard of Oz*, Dorothy doesn't receive a medal, a diploma or a testimonial. She doesn't get anything from the magician's black bag.

But what she learns, probably just exactly in that short moment between the Wizard leaving and Glinda the Good Witch showing up, is that she never actually lost the opportunity to make her remarkable desires come true. Everything she has wished for has always been right there in front of her all along. She doesn't need to look any further than her own backyard, because, as she says so wonderfully, "if it isn't there, I never really lost it to begin with."

Most people miss the biggest opportunities because they hustle so hard to create remarkable moments. They miss seeing the opportunities which are almost always dressed as pauses between the unremarkable moments.

If only we can learn how to see them.

So, take a moment. Read this book. You'll see. You're off to see the wizard. The wonderful wizard of pause.

Robert Rose
Los Angeles, California

"But, they have one thing

you haven't got…"

THE WIZARD OF OZ

PROLOGUE

A Manifesto for 21st-Century Brand Building

IT'S AUGUST 24, 2013. You're on vacation in Paris, France. Like 10 million other tourists who pass through the City of Light each year, you stop by to wander through the largest and most visited art museum in the world.

On this scorching summer day, you try to avoid eye contact with armed troops roaming the grounds, sweating it out in full battle fatigues. Family in tow, you take up position in the queue that forms before the iconic, glass-ensconced pyramid structure that sits in front of the building.

Once inside, you stroll the hallways and corridors with thousands of others—not knowing really what to look for other than one piece of art in particular. There are upward of 35,000 paintings, artifacts and objects on display over 782,910 square feet at the Louvre, but only *one* exhibit is universally recognized as the highest standard of its class. It's not the biggest painting in the building or, one could argue, even the most majestic. Art aficionados often point to other masterpieces worthy of much greater attention than this one, which measures 30 by 21 inches, weighs 18 pounds and was created sometime in the early 16th century.

This is the *only* painting among thousands that is certain to pull the masses toward her. Like an invisible magnet, she gently attracts rapt attention from swarms of curious humans, who file up to take a closer look and jostle for prime selfie positions.

In a single word, she is, quite frankly, *irresistible*.

By now, you already know the name of the painting in question.

The Original Source Code

Leonardo Da Vinci's masterpiece was described by *The Independent* as "the best known, most visited, most written about, most parodied work of art in the world." The *Mona Lisa* holds the Guinness World Record for the highest known insurance valuation in history, pegged at $100 million in December 1962. Considered priceless, she was gifted by Da Vinci to King Francis I of France and is now property of the French Republic, on permanent display at the Louvre—with a few interruptions—since 1797.

But, up until now, few have dug deep enough to explain the most intriguing and relevant story of all—especially as it relates to the art and science of influencing positive buyer behavior.

What if the real story behind the fame of the *Mona Lisa* is the first clue to cracking the ultimate marketing code? Could Da Vinci's masterpiece be a key that unlocks magical, mystical forces that generate unusually high volumes of customer attention, investor interest, talent attraction, reputational equity, public goodwill and overall net worth? What if her story holds timeless secrets you could employ to build a business and brand that becomes, quite frankly, irresistible?

Take a moment to reflect on your own personal fascinations and purchasing decisions. Why do you watch certain movies, buy certain brands of coffee, cheer for certain sports teams or athletes, follow certain personalities or visit certain places? When was the last time you seriously pondered how you (or anyone) can make that split-second decision whenever you encounter a product, person, place, event or object you find to be undeniably *irresistible*?

Simply Irresistible?

The origins of the word "irresistible" date back to the 1590s and the Latin word *irresistibilis*. For centuries, humankind has danced with this word—and the feelings it inspires—in a million different ways. The job offer or promotion that's too good to turn down. The temptress who beckons. The tantalizingly sweet chocolate, silky smooth whiskey or adoringly cute puppy in the window that's impossible to resist. Whispers to your soul of a spiritual calling you can't ignore.

As partners in business, life and crime, Dana Zilic and I are endlessly fascinated by the undercurrents of human behavior. What makes people tick, makes them behave in the way they do? Since that late August afternoon in Paris as we watched the hordes flock and gawk, the *Mona Lisa* has become for us a metaphorical symbol for a different kind of fascination. After much rumination, we realized that Da Vinci's painting symbolized and represented something much more than a famous and priceless piece of art.

The Louvre was originally commissioned as a fortress by King Philip II in 1190, but what if today it stands as the perfect metaphor for any overcrowded, hyper-competitive market—including yours? Those 35,000 works of art are struggling to be worthy of public attention, just like any brand or product in any other overly congested, hotly contested sector. In many respects, the Louvre is a lot like North America's 55,500 supermarkets that stock about 40,000 items on their respective shelves. It's like the 48,000 realtors battling for listings in bustling cities like Toronto or the 45,210 lawyers in Cook County, Illinois, who are hustling for cases. Whether it's the grocery store you visit weekly, the home you're trying to sell or the attorney you suddenly need, countless product and service vendors are hoping that, when you do make a choice, you will choose them.

Examine your own competitive landscape. How much does it mirror those daily dynamics at the Louvre? In that light, the *Mona Lisa* could be viewed as a Holy Grail for anyone who aspires to create top-of-mind awareness: a metaphorical goddess for those who dream of building and being part of a brand deemed worthy above all others.

With respect, admiration and accolades to iconic brands such as Disney, Ferrari, Nike and everyone from Harley-Davidson to Harvard and Harry Potter, *Big Little Legends* follows a different path. This book explores the real-life stories of otherwise ordinary, everyday leaders who accomplished extraordinary results and established long-term legacies. Plenty of business books have already been published that provide great detail on how giants like Apple, Amazon, Ford, Facebook, Google or Tesla achieved greatness. These tales of commercial triumph often revolve around the exploits of gifted, entrepreneurial geniuses or immortals of industry that regular people can hardly relate to. Not everyone readily identifies with the likes of Jobs, Musk or Bezos.

In taking an alternative route, *Big Little Legends* focuses on studying irresistible brands from an entirely different perspective. What if we examined this subject through the eyes and real-life experiences of mere mortals? In other words, what if we turned the lens on people similar to us?

It is through these stories that you are about to discover your own Rosetta Stone of contemporary brand building. A new code and covenant that puts an end to the undignified and utter nonsense of spamming, interrupting, prodding and begging for people to become your customers. Instead of asking "how do we get noticed?" why not ask "how do we become *worthy* of attention?" This is why a deeper understanding of the *Mona Lisa* and her enduring appeal is relevant to what you are trying to accomplish. In many respects, she opens a window of possibilities that few in your competitive space will even bother to examine. Possibilities like:

- What if you could focus your marketing efforts on creating an organic "pull" instead of a manufactured "push"?

- What if you adopted a proactive, long-term approach to brand building instead of the reactive demands of short-term pitching and promoting?

- What if you knew there was a way to firmly ensconce your brand as a "Category of One" for decades to come?

The dynamics of every single type of commercial activity changes *dramatically* when the customer comes to you.

We call it the Mona Lisa Effect.

Functioning like a giant magnet on steroids, the Mona Lisa Effect is vividly exemplified in famous companies, personalities, brands, events and landmarks that enjoy the same hypnotic power of attraction that the painting embodies itself. Evidence of the Mona Lisa Effect can be witnessed in the behavior of the more than 800,000 bikers who converge each year on Sturgis, South Dakota; the mobs of visitors who kiss a certain fabled—and most unhygienic— stone at Blarney Castle in Cork, Ireland; or the upward of 300,000 pilgrims who set out each year to follow the Camino, that spiritual path that leads to Santiago de Compostela in northern Spain. It reveals itself when visitors to Philadelphia clamor for a selfie or photo op with a statue of a fictitious pugilist or when London tourists risk life and limb in busy traffic to mimic a popular album cover at a crosswalk on Abbey Road.

The Mona Lisa Effect explains the long lines in the hot Florida sun for amusement park rides at Disney, the hundreds of sweaty strangers waiting to buy an Apple phone or the combined 28 million subscribers (as of 2020) eagerly consuming thousands of videos produced by YouTube sensations such as Casey Neistat, Gary Vaynerchuk or Lilly Singh.

By the same token, the Mona Lisa Effect can also be witnessed at dozens of crowded and wildly popular small businesses that sell otherwise ordinary products, such as a certain New Orleans coffee shop or a certain Seattle fish market. This dynamic also unfolds at a Las Vegas pawn shop that lures up to 5,000 visitors daily, or the burger joint on a remote stretch of Northern Ontario highway with its never-ending lineups that form like clockwork each summer. Either by intention or accident, these brands have tapped into the magic of the Mona Lisa Effect, taking on their own special aura of mystique and magnetism to become dominant, top-of-mind players in their space.

Ultimately, every serious brand builder aspires to create their own Mona Lisa Effect. It's like winning the marketing version of the Nobel Prize or the Super Bowl, with a brand reputation ballooning to the point where eager customers line up in droves, ravenous to buy at any price you set. It's tangible proof that buyer behavior has been heavily tilted in your favor. And, thanks to the power of the internet, this approach does *not* require deep pockets, access to venture capital, an army of experts or a huge outlay of advertising dollars.

Through the unblinking eyes and first-hand experiences of *Big Little Legends*, you will see with stunning clarity how other leaders—not much different from you—have accomplished exactly this. As you begin with the story of Mona Lisa herself, consider this book as a manual of applied history: an exploration of past events and a clear understanding of our present-day circumstances—and how they both shape our future.

A warning: if you choose to keep reading and plunge into the murky, bottomless waters of what makes an iconic brand come to life, there's a chance you may never swim back to safer shores. Your perceptions and ideas about marketing may be forever altered. Should you make the leap, prepare to feast on a literary buffet unapologetically stuffed like a plump Thanksgiving turkey with metaphors, symbols and timeless secrets that reveal how irresistible brands are built by everyday leaders just like you in any sector or category— from anywhere in the world.

Bon appétit!

*All our knowledge has
its origins in our perceptions.*

LEONARDO DA VINCI

PART I

WHAT'S YOUR STORY ?

1

DRIVE DEMAND LIKE DA VINCI

Inspire Attraction Through the Art of the Steal

March 6, 2012

Michael had no clue how much his entire world—and the bladed buying habits of millions—would change that day.

With one click of a button.

Prior to that moment, Michael Dubin had invested every nickel he could get his hands on and a metric ton of sweat equity, but there was no way of knowing with certainty what would occur once he pushed that "upload" button. All he knew for sure was that he felt proud of his work. And that his simple idea was a risk worth betting on.

The idea itself came unwrapped at a Christmas party in December 2010. Michael was chatting with his friend's father-in-law and heard about how the man needed to unload a warehouse stocked with surplus razor blades after a business deal went sour. Commiserating over holiday cocktails, they shared common frustrations with the blade-purchasing process: the pain of hunting down indifferent clerks and practically begging them to open an acrylic-encased "razor fortress"—and paying a king's ransom for the privilege.

Michael started thinking. *What if I could eliminate the expense and hassle of buying razor blades? What if blades just showed up at your door each month for a simple, affordable price?*

Within a week, he had registered a domain name. He quit his salaried job to work on the concept full-time. Could he bring the idea to life? From a bootstrapped operation out of his tiny apartment, Michael launched a beta site in 2011, but knew he also needed to attract attention. Working with a friend, he spent months whittling down a four-page video script to the point where every moment and every frame had a specific reason for being. Michael wanted the video's first punch to land hard, but struggled to find the perfect catch-phrase. Until his friend Lucia Aniello blurted out: "Our blades are f**king great."

At 6 a.m. Pacific on March 6, 2012, Michael uploaded a 90-second video on YouTube that altered the marketing universe forever.

And a Big Little Legend was born.

Boom!

What appeared to be an on-the-fly, homemade spot was, in truth, a highly planned effort—one that only cost $4,500 to make. With co-conspirator Lucia, Michael shot the video over one day in a warehouse borrowed from a friend. Within 48 hours of the video going live, Dollar Shave Club processed 12,000 orders—clearing out the warehouse and crashing the company's website. Three months later, the hilariously disruptive video had racked up nearly 5 million views, and the company achieved sales of $3 million by the end of 2012. By 2013 it was $19 million. The next year it was $65 million. The irresistible appeal of the DSC brand was worth a princely sum on the open market and on July 19, 2016, the company was sold to Unilever for the handsome price of $1 billion.

Michael Dubin and the story of Dollar Shave Club is a vivid example of what the Mona Lisa Effect looks like for 21st-century brand builders. An otherwise ordinary product becomes wildly popular, acquiring legions of customers without the owner having to fork over a fortune for traditional marketing and advertising. When Michael pressed the upload button on YouTube on March 6, 2012, there were no guarantees that multiple waves of fervent customers would be rolling in, sharing his video with millions of other web surfers and disturbing his deep-pocketed, well-armed enemy.

Procter & Gamble never saw the storm coming.

The Mona Lisa Effect in Modern-Day Marketing

When Dollar Shave Club appeared seemingly out of nowhere in 2012, Gillette dominated the razor blade market with a staggering 72% market share. Purchased by P&G for $57 billion in 2005, Gillette was the proverbial Goliath: a ten-foot-tall, 800-pound gorilla in a product category considered disruption-proof in every way. Since uploading that first video, Michael Dubin has become akin to a business rock star, inspiring other scrappy Davids to aim their slingshots at stuffy suits dominating status quo territories of marketing and distribution. Constantly asked to pose for selfies while hustling through airports, Michael stepped aside as CEO in January 2021 with his legacy secure. By the year of his 40th birthday, he had become senior advisor at a growing company with over 600 employees and more than 4 million subscribers.

The DSC story is fascinating on many levels. The central character—Michael—had never owned a company before, never sat down to build a marketing plan or create new global distribution channels. He didn't know anything about securing venture capital, building a customer fulfillment center or making YouTube videos. There was no carefully scripted business plan that could have predicted how a five-year-old start-up would achieve a ten-figure exit while beating a behemoth like Procter & Gamble at their own marketing game by inventing a new one altogether.

Was it just a fluke?

Did Michael just happen to get lucky? Was this simply a case of having the right product on the right platform at the right time?

Or did Dollar Shave Club simply reach into the pages of history and adopt a timeless blueprint for any leader who has ever hoped to stand out and attract attention in an overcrowded, noisy world?

That blueprint begins with a deeper understanding and application of a gift we first acquired as kids when we were getting tucked into bed at night. It dates back to when we learned to recite nursery rhymes and became absorbed by riveting accounts like "Little Red Riding Hood" or "The Three Little Pigs." This timeless art is our shared human birthright: the oldest, most compelling form of communication our world has ever known. The single spark that lights the fire of intimacy, heals human suffering and inspires personal change, global movements and millions of customers to choose a specific item like a new razor blade. Explore the origin of any legend—from King Arthur to Robin Hood, Honest Abe, the Babe, JFK; from MLK to the Wonderful World of Disney, Apple, Nike, Oprah and Dollar Shave Club—and you'll see with stunning clarity how a single strand of our shared genetic code is hardwired into the DNA of the greatest brands in history.

Storytelling.

It's that simple.

Building an irresistible brand that detonates the chain reaction we describe as the Mona Lisa Effect always begins with a simple story.

And it has nothing—repeat, nothing—to do with the quality or merits of your product or service.

It has everything to do with two key factors:

1   The story you are going to tell.
2   The story that others are going to tell about you.

I have never met Michael Dubin in person, but have studied and followed his story closely since he first appeared on branding radar screens in March 2012. Originally from Philadelphia, he was a struggling history major at Emory University in Atlanta before taking an entry-level marketing job in New York. On a whim, he studied sketch comedy with an improv group called the Upright Citizens Brigade, practicing the art form for about eight years with no end goal. Although he had no desire to become a stand-up comedian, Michael was fascinated and learned as much as he could about the craft before that holiday conversation with his buddy's father-in-law in 2010.

Lady Luck shows up when preparation collides with opportunity, and Dame Fortune was smiling broadly when Dollar Shave Club's inaugural video was uploaded to the internet. What followed was 1:33 of exaggerated, attention-grabbing madcap silliness that also extolled the features of DSC razors. After that explosive F-bomb opening, Michael takes us on a zany warehouse tour that includes scenes with a tennis racket, a toddler shaving a man's head, polio jokes, a machete, a clumsy bear mascot, a happy immigrant worker and a giant American flag. In other words, DSC did not follow a well-worn, beaten-down marketing path promoting the virtues of "quality, selection and service," "affordable and reliable" or "cleaner, whiter, brighter."

Michael simply told a story.

One that real people could relate to, make sense of and rally around.

In the same way people rallied more than a century ago around the unlikely story of a certain painting that suddenly disappeared from a Paris museum.

A portrait of a mysterious woman now protected by a well-monitored, ultra-secure, bulletproof glass casing. Aside from a few interruptions, like the COVID-19 pandemic of 2020, this object from the 16th century has consistently exerted a magnetic pull on the marketplace, similar to what occurred when online shoppers crashed the internet with open wallets and credit cards for DSC products.

So, why exactly is the *Mona Lisa* regarded as the hands-down, undisputed most famous painting in the world? Is it her enigmatic smile? The mystery surrounding her true identity? Does it have anything to do with the fact that she was

painted by the ultimate rock god of the Italian Renaissance—
the Vitruvian Wonder himself—Mr. Leonardo Da Vinci?

The answer is none of the above.

The mesmerizing appeal of the *Mona Lisa* has little or
nothing to with either the quality of the work or reputation
of the artist. Closer investigation reveals a specific moment
in time when her brand was changed forever by an astonishing "whodunit" crime story.

How *Mona Lisa* Went Viral

The sudden popularity of Leonardo's masterpiece cannot be
explained by either conventional wisdom or by modern data
and analytics. In the same manner as DSC, however, there
were events and circumstances that clarify precisely how the
Mona Lisa became a cultural icon—the slam-dunk, top-of-
mind, most prominent work of art the world has ever known.

First, a few pertinent facts.

Questions persist over the actual name of Leonardo's
model. Most historians agree that it's a portrait of Lisa Ghe-
rardini, wife of a wealthy silk merchant named Francesco
del Giocondo. Why Giocondo never kept the painting he
commissioned is unclear, but it was later delivered by Leonardo himself to the king of France. Up until the 20th century,
the *Mona Lisa* was largely unknown to the general public.
Hardly anyone outside of art society circles even knew of
her existence. In fact, an 1880 publication about the Louvre
showered more attention on Leonardo's other masterpiece,
The Last Supper.

But, one Monday morning in Paris, a singular act of brazen skullduggery changed everything for this otherwise small, ordinary and unassuming portrait.

On August 21, 1911, the *Mona Lisa* was stolen from the Louvre.

It was an inside job.

On that Monday morning when the Louvre was closed for its weekly cleaning, an Italian craftsman who had once worked at the museum simply walked through the door with the other workers. Seeing no one was around, he took *Mona Lisa* from the wall, removed it from its frame and wrapped it in the smock he was wearing. Once the coast was clear, he and *Mona Lisa* walked out in broad daylight.

The 29-year-old man—Vincenzo Peruggia—smuggled the painting home to his Paris apartment. For well over 24 hours, not one of the high-ranking officials at the museum even knew the painting was missing. When they finally did notice, they called in the authorities. After the Paris police announced the theft, newspapers all over the world ran headlines about the missing masterpiece.

Shock and outrage followed. "Unimaginable" screamed one French headline. "60 Detectives Seek Stolen 'Mona Lisa,' French Public Indignant!" blared the *New York Times*. Other stories appeared in *Le Petit Journal*, the *Daily Mail* and newspapers all over the globe.

The heist quickly became an international scandal. Prominent suspects were interrogated, including Picasso and American tycoon turned art collector J.P. Morgan. Conspiracy theories ran rampant. Was the heavily mustachioed Kaiser Wilhelm II of Germany behind it all? Were the authorities bungling the investigation? Why did the chief of police in Paris suddenly retire?

It was the best publicity no amount of money could buy.

Millions upon millions of dollars' worth of free advertising and PR were generated daily by newspapers from Toronto to Tokyo, Toledo and Timbuktu. At the time, local newspapers were the equivalent of Facebook, Twitter or Google. They were the only platform that could distribute information to mass audiences. In effect, the *Mona Lisa* was the beneficiary of a 100% free-of-charge global marketing push. It was the first major property crime to receive international media coverage, making it the best viral ad campaign for any work of art in history.

Almost overnight, a painting known only to insiders became universally recognized through catchy headlines, reams of dramatic copy and front-page photos of her bewitching smile.

When the press coverage first exploded, that's when lineups began to form. After closing for a week, the museum re-opened to a waiting mob. Curious and shocked Parisians descended on the Louvre just to view the empty wall she once occupied. They left flowers, notes of condolences and wishes for a speedy return. The public display of grief was comparable to what happened globally after the tragic 1997 Paris auto accident that claimed the life of Princess Diana.

Meanwhile, the incessant media glare forced Peruggia underground as he laid low in his Paris apartment. A little more than two years after snatching the *Mona Lisa*, Peruggia returned to his native country and attempted to sell the portrait to a high-end art dealer who consulted with the director at the Uffizi Gallery. The two men became suspicious and called the police. The next day, Peruggia was under arrest. Mystery solved. Case closed.

At trial, Peruggia claimed he was an Italian patriot, trying to return *Mona Lisa* to her rightful home—he was under the impression it had been stolen from Italy by Napoleon. The court rejected this argument and, after pleading guilty to theft, Peruggia spent eight months in jail before resuming a life of obscurity.

But from the moment the painting was recovered, the international media machine had kicked back into high gear. The good news about her safe recovery once again placed her beguiling image on front pages everywhere. *Mona Lisa*'s glorious return in 1913 could be compared to a modern-day tour of the Royal Family. After a series of public exhibitions in Italy, arrangements were made for her triumphant return to Paris. When she came back to the Louvre and was restored to her proper place, the size of the crowd that came to see her was estimated at 120,000.

She may have left the Louvre wrapped in Peruggia's smock as a competent work of art, but her dramatic return transformed her into a larger-than-life national treasure. Leonardo's portrait of an enigmatic Florentine woman became the world's first art icon for the masses—a cultural legend and commercial sensation that endures to this day. In her era, she was like Elvis, the Beatles and Beyoncé all rolled into one. Critics and art lovers who had initially held zero interest in the painting began weighing in with high-brow opinions, debating and endlessly analyzing *Mona Lisa*'s mystifying smile. The interest continues to this day, making her the #1 jewel in the Louvre's crown. She alone is the brand magnet that attracts over 10 million visitors a year while being immortalized through pop culture.

But, what would have transpired if the pilfering Peruggia had snatched a different painting that fateful August day? Would massive crowds still flock to the Louvre, buying souvenirs and snapping selfies with the *Mona Lisa*? According to writer and filmmaker Joe Medeiros, director of the award-winning documentary *Mona Lisa Is Missing*, perhaps not. "From the time Leonardo painted her, she's always had a certain fame and mystique," said Medeiros, former head writer of *The Tonight Show with Jay Leno* and now considered to be the leading authority on Vincenzo Peruggia and his unthinkable theft. "Peruggia didn't steal the *Mona Lisa* because she was fairly well known. He took her because the portrait was small and easily carried. Once she disappeared, her fame exploded—because, like the song says, you don't know what you've got till it's gone."

Imagine for a moment if Peruggia had walked away with another one of Leonardo's works on that August day, or another great work by a different painter altogether. If that had happened, then it would have been *that* image that became ever-present on our T-shirts and Warhol prints and trinkets and memes. The incredible story of the unlikely heist of the *Mona Lisa* and the immense media coverage that followed is what skyrocketed the work's appeal and made it a household name.

A Marketing Snowball Becomes an Avalanche

Dollar Shave Club was not the first company to sell razor blades through the internet. Leonardo's portrait was not the first painting to be displayed at the Louvre. What DSC and the story of the *Mona Lisa* reveal is that the undisputed champion in any market is not necessarily the first brand to step into the competitive arena, but instead the one that becomes entrenched as the top-of-mind choice. In that respect, it wasn't the quality or performance of the actual razor blades that commanded a billion-dollar buyout for DSC. It also wasn't the quality of the actual "art" that made *Mona Lisa* a legend.

Attracting attention and driving demand like Da Vinci hinges on a simple, powerful truth. In both cases, DSC and the *Mona Lisa* became metaphorical, story-based snowballs that kept rolling downhill. Once an initial push has been made, the human fascination for gripping drama and our instinctive urge to share captivating stories have the potential to create an avalanche of marketing momentum that becomes unstoppable. In what we now call the "attention economy," leaders are shifting away from paying for content that relies on traditional media to deliver messages to mass audiences (newspapers, magazines, radio, TV networks) and are instead creating their own content and communities through social media platforms such as Facebook, Twitter, LinkedIn and YouTube.

Attention is two things at once:

1   A form of currency
2   A limited resource

Let's tackle point #2 first. Attention is a resource because you, the reader, only have so much of it. The economist Herbert A. Simon coined the phrase "attention economy" in 1972, arguing that attention was the "bottleneck of human thought," limiting where we can selectively shift our focus and what we can act on. In the digital age, the dizzying wealth of information we're subjected to has created a poverty of attention as we all drive like data drunkards at the speed of light.

That's not how it was in the horse-and-wagon days of Leonardo, when access to information was severely limited. During the period of the Renaissance, many people could not read and write. Education was a luxury. Today, access to information is readily available to anyone with an internet connection. And that brings us back to point #1. Attention equals currency. As users, we pay for free content with our attention. As marketers, we are challenged to find ways to have users spend more time with us and ignore the daily deluge of digital stimuli that ranges from cute puppies on roller skates to casserole recipes, fashion trends, celebrity gossip and 24/7 breaking news. Created by Tim Berners-Lee in 1989, the web ranks with the discovery of fire, the printing press, the automobile, radio, electricity, the Fender Stratocaster, the iPhone, Oreo cookies, Frosted Flakes and M&M's. Thanks to the internet, the previously unimaginable ability to create and share fascinating stories that attract attention, drive demand and boost brand value has opened an enormous gulf between those who will grow and prosper and those who are destined to wither and die.

To be sure, the web wields a ruthless, double-edged sword. On the one hand, it has decapitated thousands of companies, entrepreneurs, realtors, consultants, mortgage brokers, small businesses and sales professionals who refused to see the looming threat posed by Amazon, Shopify, eBay and any number of online marketplaces, mobile apps and livestreaming services. The global pandemic of 2020 only served to further expose individuals and organizations lacking in digital fluency and agility, unable to leverage competitive advantages provided by the internet.

On the other hand, the web is a profitable haven for any leader who is ready, willing and able to earn attention by sharpening their storytelling ax. Sudden notoriety, colossal success and massive market share achieved by Dollar Shave Club, the *Mona Lisa* and other Big Little Legends demands more than trumpeting the table stakes merits of the actual product or service.

Decoding the Art of the Steal

Capturing and holding audience attention while converting it into currency always depends to a large degree on something so simple—yet razor sharp in terms of its timeless relevance.

The widespread universal appeal and electrifying human energy created by the power of *storytelling*.

For centuries, our capacity to absorb and share stories has been one of the few aspects of the human experience that has withstood all manner of social, cultural, political, environmental and technological change. As celebrated Canadian author Margaret Atwood explains, "You're never going to kill storytelling, because it's built in the human plan. We come with it." To be sure, the floodgates of audience fascination opened for *Mona Lisa* once the unrelenting wave of publicity following her theft washed over millions the world over. Leonardo's painting was the lucky beneficiary of a story that *happened* to it. It was like a lottery score. Winning the branding sweepstakes through outside events.

Michael Dubin and Dollar Shave Club carefully *crafted and created* their own story, using time-honored techniques to infuse dramatic elements such as identifying a hero, the innate desire of that hero and an obstacle or villain that needed to be overcome. Whether a story is thrust upon you by external forces or you develop and share it from within, it's crucial to understand that storytelling is the conceptual bedrock on which to develop any magnetically irresistible brand.

Timeless Takeaways

#1. A story either happens to you . . . or you make one happen. You can be *reactive* and wait for a story to be dropped into your lap. Or you can be *proactive* and grab that metaphorical Red Bull by the horns. Leaders who understand their role in creating Strategic Drama will recognize their responsibility for initiating a story.

It is possible to sit, wait and hope for a stroke of incredible dumb marketing luck, like a certain soup vendor in Manhattan who gained heaping, overflowing amounts of customer attention following one 1995 episode of *Seinfeld*. More than likely, though, you will need to become your own executive producer. What if you borrowed influences from Shakespeare, Broadway and Hollywood and staged your own production, the way DSC did? Could your personal story possess the potential to burst open the dams and create an overflow of customers? What if you started seriously pondering what needs to occur to trigger the Mona Lisa Effect for your brand?

#2. Art without a story is just paint on a canvas.

A business without a story is just like every other business. That explains why a Paris museum is the perfect metaphor for any overcrowded market. Like thousands of other paintings hanging in the Louvre, your business or organization runs the risk of delivering a world-class product or service, yet still winding up ignored by the market while one intriguing competitor draws all the attention.

#3. People will be willing accomplices in your story.

Ever wonder why complete strangers leave flowers, notes, candles, stuffed animals and artwork for people they've never met? From the untimely, tragic deaths of John Lennon, Princess Diana, Prince, George Floyd and many others, we have witnessed how profoundly people are impacted by a story—even if they have no direct relationship to the victim. But it's not only tragedy that evokes such reactions. Each year, people make pilgrimages to Fenway Park, Graceland, the Grassy Knoll, Route 66, Alcatraz, Loch Ness or the Taj Mahal, or go out of their way to wait in line for a bowl of soup in Midtown from a real-life soup vendor who was the inspiration for a fictional sitcom character.

When DSC's YouTube debut was uploaded in March 2012, Michael Dubin had no inkling how many strangers would pay homage to his own timeless art of the "steel," watching, sharing and commenting on his video 30 million times over. The power of his original story grabbed attention and created a connection that moves people to action. It became the emotional conduit that made people feel like they could see themselves in the story and become actually involved and immersed in it.

The Dénouement

Our research involving more than 2,000 seminar attendees confirms what legends are really made of. When asked for a list of human qualities to describe individuals they view as legendary, people at our seminars and events have singled out traits such as decisiveness, determination, self-motivation, conviction, confidence, adaptability, positivity, bravery, honesty and scores of others. What's most revealing, however, are two qualities never mentioned by any audience member. The first is money. No one ever suggests that you need to be flush with cash to become legendary. In other words, success has much less to do with your financial means, and much more to do with your level of emotional grit and creative mettle.

The second is education. From the sounds of it, people don't seem to care if you have an Oxford or Harvard degree. They're not swayed in the least by any string of impressive letters or professional designations that follows your name on a business card or LinkedIn profile.

You don't need to wait for mountains of venture capital or academic pieces of paper. You can "Be Like Mike" and move forward right now with the leadership decision to stand apart from the crowd. Nowhere is it carved in stone that you must follow the herd, lumbering along familiar, predictable marketing paths marked "average" in your category. History reveals that not all brands are created equal, but it has little to do with the size of your company, product quality, service delivery, graphic design, geography or number of years in business.

As a leader, you can determine a route of your own choosing.

You can make a choice with incomplete information, discover who you really are—beyond your product and service offerings—and build a story-based brand that loyal fans will find irresistible. You can apply the wisdom of existential philosopher Jean-Paul Sartre, who observed, "Man is always a teller of tales, he lives surrounded by his stories and the stories of others. He sees everything that happens to him through them; and he tries to live his life as if he were recounting it."

You alone can understand that stories offer much more than entertainment value. You can ditch traditional marketing language and make a bigger-picture, strategic connection between storytelling and human desire, motivation and action.

Next, we explore the real-life genesis of a Big Little Legend. From the most unlikely of categories, we'll wander to the other side of the tracks and discover how creating Strategic Drama fostered one of Canada's most enduring and endearing small business success stories.

*I don't think there's any one playbook
out there in front of us that we should be
following. You can take a little piece from
Starbucks; you can take a little piece
from Nike; you can take a little piece from
Apple. You have to keep your eyes
open and learn from others
that have traveled the path before.*

MICHAEL DUBIN

2

START YOUR STORY ENGINE

The Branding Spark That Lights a Fire

September 18, 2006

Radio listeners in Fredericton, New Brunswick, had never heard commercials like these.

In two decades as a professional broadcaster, I had never heard anything like them either.

And it was my voice they were listening to.

Launched on September 18, 2006, this series of highly original radio ads reflected an unconventional marketing strategy that ventured along an unfamiliar path. Jim and his wife, Dawna, owners of a small family business, had taken traditional advertising wisdom and heaved it out the window. With no guarantees of success, they started playing a completely different game, with short spots that made no mention of their products, prices or promotions. Almost overnight, Jim and Dawna Gilbert changed the entire direction of their otherwise ordinary independent business with a collection of audio vignettes that didn't sound like anything else in their town, or even in the entire country.

What Fredericton audiences heard on their radios were a series of 30-second stories about "Canada's Huggable Car Dealer."

As Jim remembers: "I was apprehensive about those first ads, especially since they didn't talk about cars or prices. They just told fun-loving stories about me being the Casanova of Customer Focus, the Romeo of Roadsters or the McDreamy of Drive. We talked about how people could stop by for a daily dose of 'Hugtonium' and boost their love affair with their car, and their libido! Those spots quickly created a sharp contrast between us and what the public perceived as loud-talking, fast-walking, plaid-wearing, Herb Tarlek hustlers."

Building a brand reputation around the word "Huggable" really got the town talking. Within six weeks, Jim and Dawna knew they had discovered a marketing unicorn. People began approaching them at hockey games, shopping malls and coffee shops to compliment them on their ads. Strangers went out of their way to walk up to Jim and ask for a hug. The Gilberts didn't know it at the time, but those random encounters were the early warning signs of the Mona Lisa Effect. Something magically magnetic was about to materialize.

And that's when Dawna experienced an epiphany.

She realized they could turn this embryonic idea into something more than just a clever radio campaign. If she and Jim and their small team could fully embrace it, the "Huggable" story could become the focal point for their entire brand. Dawna knew that she and Jim had to go all-in. If they didn't, the public would see it as just another here-today, gone-tomorrow gimmicky advertising ploy.

If Walt Disney himself could have re-imagined what a used car lot might look like, he would have been proud to serve as Chief Imagineer at Jim Gilbert's Wheels & Deals—Canada's Huggable Car Dealer. Trusting instinct and intuition, the Gilberts unknowingly embarked on an uncertain journey destined to create what we call Strategic Drama. What began with a series of story-based radio commercials quickly mushroomed into a branding powerhouse, a word-of-mouth force of nature supported by hundreds of ever-present stuffed teddy bears—along with upward of 101 other items that capture the spirit of what a "Huggable" car dealership is about. Along with colorful bears, visitors will see merry-go-rounds, furry mascots, a 1.2-mile nature trail, free popcorn, children's books, an online channel focused on "Motorvational" stories and much, much more.

The results have been nothing short of staggering.

Since discovering their uniquely original story in 2006, Canada's Huggable Car Dealer has experienced phenomenal business growth. Over time, Wheels & Deals has eventually become the largest independent used car dealership in all four Atlantic Canadian provinces, with sales numbers and profitability margins that defy logic.

Defying logic is exactly what Jim and Dawna Gilbert have been doing since day one.

In the Beginning

In 1979, small-town Jim set out to take on the world in a big-time way. Just out of high school, he met his bride-to-be and together they opened a combination gas station/used car lot on the corner of a tiny village just outside of Fredericton.

Their start-up inventory consisted of one car and two gas pumps, backed by a $10,000 bank loan.

By the time Jim and I met in the fall of 2002, he was situated on a small lot on the city's north side. With Dawna working shoulder-to-shoulder in the trenches alongside him, Jim worked for nearly two decades, slowly gaining ground inch by inch. Cash flow was a constant issue. Jim and Dawna depended on each sale to buy more vehicle inventory, make payroll and stay one step ahead of their creditors. Run ragged on the small business treadmill, they frequently struggled to keep their financial heads above water.

No matter how many extra miles they traveled to take care of their customers, Jim and Dawna also felt stifled by negative perceptions of their industry. They could feel the cloud of invisible judgment when new acquaintances learned they owned a used car lot. Deep down in their hearts, Jim and Dawna knew they weren't anything like the greasy, fast-talking, fly-by-night hustlers that folks were visualizing in their minds. They took a different approach, running a first-class operation with a clean, well-appointed building. They paid impeccable attention to detail and genuine customer care with extra warranties, follow-up phone calls and handwritten birthday notes to their customers every year. Those extra miles also included donating uniforms and equipment for kids in local hockey, baseball and soccer leagues. They constantly searched for new ways to create a healthy workplace culture and invested in professional development for their people. The citizens of Fredericton, however, did not see all that effort—to them, Wheels & Deals was no different from every other used car dealer. Despite their tangible efforts, they still got tagged with that slick and quick, tricky and icky label. Whether they liked it or not, the Gilberts were being schooled on how the power of perception shapes our reality.

I know what I was visualizing about used car dealers on the day Jim introduced himself at a local Chamber of Commerce function. But when that shy, soft-spoken gentleman presented me with his business card—it was a foreshadowing of things to come. A single phrase on the card said it all.

> The glow of one warm thought means more to me than anything. Thank you!

I did a quick mental double-take. The card struck me as peculiar, maybe even a little kumbaya—especially when you consider that 93% of the public considers Jim's profession to be the least trustworthy among all others. Lower on the credibility scale than lawyers, politicians and marketers. At the time of our initial meeting, Jim and Dawna had five full-time employees and one part-timer. In effect, they were like many other small mom-and-pop businesses— selling interchangeable, ordinary products, generating about $1.5 million in annual revenue.

From that day, Jim, Dawna and the Wheels & Deals team embarked on a shared journey to develop their professional sales and customer service skills. Over a four-year period, we conducted monthly sessions at the dealership and focused our efforts on "soft skills" training designed to improve the overall customer experience. Slowly, sales began improving, but we also started pondering if there were more effective ways to get people to visit their lot in the first place. Improved sales skills could be an exponential multiplier if more prospects could be encouraged to stop in for a visit.

Jim had often wondered about the effectiveness of established advertising methods. After pumping thousands of dollars annually into radio and newspaper ads, he and Dawna began questioning the value of campaigns that made them look and sound like everybody else. Stop and think about it: take a moment to reflect on the tone of the advertising you see and hear from used car dealerships in your area. Do they tend to look and sound something like this?

Hurry on over to Citywide Used Cars and find the best deals in town. 0.9% financing on all makes and models. No credit? No problem! Our super friendly sales team is here with the biggest inventory and the best quality vehicles! Better selection, better prices, better value, better service . . . Everything's just better at Citywide Used Cars!!!

In September of 2006, that all changed when Jim, Dawna and I stumbled upon a strategic marketing approach that few others were aware of or would even attempt to try. Only much later would we learn we had accidently adopted similar principles that had garnered worldwide fame for Leonardo Da Vinci's alluring portrait and Michael Dubin's provocative razor blades. In a curious twist of fate, the Gilberts and I had picked up on a flickering hint of how we could shape a much different future for their dealership—something that was rooted in timeless lessons from the past.

A 350,000-year-old communication secret that has been embraced and relied upon by forward-thinking leaders for centuries.

With a Flick of the Switch

Dr. Polly Wiessner of the University of Utah and Arizona State University is just one of many anthropologists who have invested decades studying this secret. For the bulk of her career, Dr. Wiessner has researched hunter-gatherer societies in the jungles of Botswana, Congo and New Guinea. Her work reveals fascinating insights for anyone seeking to influence humans and buyer behavior, or to fuel trust, connection and curiosity with a discovery that can be summarized in a single, four syllable word.

Storytelling.

Stories are the DNA of human meaning. The most valued currency of collective culture or commercial enterprise. Storytelling predates the written word. It has been used for centuries to unite communities, inspire movements, create religions and send troops into battle. According to Dr. Wiessner, the moment storytelling became our most valued currency is when our ancestors learned how to fully leverage the benefits of fire.

Mass adoption of fire occurred about 350,000 years ago, and it generated much more than the capacity to cook food, stay warm and scare away predators. It also provided a central gathering spot for people to connect. The subsequent daily practice of starting a fire is what allowed our active hours to be extended. Only when fire went mainstream did humans begin gathering in groups to stoke imaginations late into the evening.

In her research of societies that have remained unchanged for thousands of years, Dr. Wiessner discovered a literal night and day difference in conversational habits. During daylight hours, hunter-gatherers devoted 65% of conversational time to matters of economics, resources, foraging strategies, supply issues, rival tribes and hunting tools, as well as the usual litany of verbal criticism, complaints, conflict and gossip involving others in the workplace.

But, when the sun goes down and the flames begin to rise...

At that moment, fully 81% of conversational time turns to exchanging tales of adventure and intrigue—the telling and re-telling of amusing, exciting escapades or endearing moments. Details are rehashed, discussed and embellished. Language itself becomes more rhythmic, complex and symbolic, taking audiences on emotional journeys filled with stunned silence, suspense, heartache or gales of laughter. In other words, until fire went mainstream, there were no stories to tell or audiences to enjoy them. People just worked, went back to a dark cave, kept to themselves and waited for the next sunrise.

A few centuries later, gifted storytellers from our species created Adam & Eve, David & Goliath, Jack & the Beanstalk and Snow White. Storytelling is how humans in every civilization have acquired a deeper understanding of each other, and how we have made sense of the world around us. That's why, 350,000 years later, hearts and minds still resonate with the words of a defiant British prime minister who swore his tiny island would "never surrender" or the stirring proclamation of a Nobel Prize–winning preacher who told Washington protestors, "I have a dream." In the late '90s, a California computer company urged us to "Think Different." It also explains why warnings from George Orwell in *1984* and the idea that "Big Brother is watching" have become increasingly relevant for 21st-century leaders concerned about technology tracking and predicting our online behavior.

Thanks to our ability to master and control fire, humanity has crafted, consumed and cherished everything from Bible stories to Broadway productions, vaudeville, TV sitcoms, soap operas, Hollywood blockbusters, *Hockey Night in Canada,* comic books, romance novels, horror flicks, the *New York Times*, Netflix originals and everything before, since and still to come. The greatest storytellers in history, from William Shakespeare to Mary Shelley, Steven Spielberg, Stephen King and Steve Jobs, all owe their very existence to our ability to extend conversational hours late into the evening.

The Magical Kingdom of Strategic Drama

After 40 years, more than 30,000 customers and over a million hugs, Jim and Dawna have fashioned a business and brand that sits on "17 Acres of Fabulous." Visitors often agree that it's the closest thing to Disney you could find at a small-town car dealership anywhere in the world. It's also a picture-perfect example of how a leader goes about the business of implementing Strategic Drama: answering the question of *who* you are—beyond the products and services you sell.

Few grasped this concept better than Walter.

In 1953, the now legendary animator spent an entire weekend drafting a five-page prospectus, hoping to secure a hefty bank loan to make his dream come true. In the memo, Walt described a magical place where "the hands of imagination will press up against the throat of reality and squeeze without mercy." He produced dazzling sketches of future attractions featuring "Alice in Wonderland" and "Cinderella."

Walt Disney offered his bankers a colorful vision and a detailed overview of an intricate city-state spanning 160 acres that would become "The Happiest Place on Earth." The location in Anaheim, California, wound up costing $17 million to build, finally opening its doors to America and the world on July 17, 1955, with a live TV special that drew almost 100 million viewers.

As a leader, Walt understood the crucial role he played in developing Strategic Drama: the *discovery*, the *telling* and the *living* of a story uniquely your own. Before the bankers opened their vaults, Walt recognized that a clearly articulated story walks hand-in-glove with a well-planned business strategy. He knew that the company story is the company strategy. An invisible force that kicks everything else into motion.

Just like Walt Disney helped his financial backer see beyond the carnival rides, Canada's Huggable Car Dealer also discovered a world of difference between listing the functional attributes and prices of a given product or service and imbuing it with something more. The real question for any leader is how to take that product or service, give it a pair of its own glass slippers and dress it up with a tantalizing story that sparks imaginations and gets people talking.

The results can be nothing short of staggering.

Since 2006 and the focused effort on living—externally and internally—the "Huggable" brand, the Gilberts have experienced phenomenal growth. By 2020, the business had grown to become a $50 million enterprise, employing 38 people while rapidly expanding into new markets. Since 2018, the Gilberts have extended their brand by offering recreational vehicles: an entirely new business unit with multiple product lines of boats, motorcycles and ATVs. Operating under the same "Huggable" brand, they battled through the 2020 global pandemic to emerge as the #1 selling dealer in the Kawasaki Canada network. In less than two years, they went straight to the top among 160 other dealerships from coast to coast.

Jim has now been profiled in multiple business books and has become something of a micro-celebrity, invited to speak at executive retreats and keynoting at business conferences. Spellbound audiences shake their heads in disbelief whenever they hear his incredible, against-the-grain, against-all-odds rags-to-riches and logic-defying story.

Many years later, the Gilberts and I also discovered we had more than just great marketing insight and history on our side.

We also had science.

Why Do People Cry at Movies?

Since the dawn of the internet, our tools of communication have changed at breakneck speed, but our human brains have not. Until recently, little has been done through the unblinking lens of neuroscience to understand the hypnotic power of story. In 2012, however, Claremont Graduate University professor and researcher Dr. Paul Zak made a landmark discovery that explains the primal, biological impact that storytelling has on humans.

Specifically, Dr. Zak wanted to know why stories have the capability to alter our beliefs, influence our behavior and affect our physiology. Why do we become anxious, afraid or weepy watching one movie, but feel joyful and blissful watching another? Through a series of experiments involving blood samples, he traced this back to a biochemical trigger called oxytocin, a chemical now described as the "love hormone." Dr. Zak discovered that oxytocin produces feelings of trust, empathy and connectedness. The release of oxytocin increases kindness, openness toward new ideas and charity toward others. It causes some to shed tears or laugh out loud while watching moving pictures on a screen. It can also prompt grown men to behave like idiots at sporting events.

Think of oxytocin as a kind of "social glue" that binds communities, or even an economic lubricant that helps grease the wheels of commerce. And this biochemical reaction is a crucial element of the Mona Lisa Effect.

In a series of experiments outlined in his 2012 book *The Moral Molecule*, Dr. Zak and his team proved that the release of oxytocin causes people to donate 50% more to a charitable cause after watching a story. They demonstrated how subjects could be influenced to give more of their precious time and energy to support political parties, animal rescue foundations, non-profit organizations like Mothers Against Drunk Driving or social movements like #BlackLivesMatter.

Dr. Zak's research confirms that storytelling is the make-or-break factor that determines which company or brand a person will buy from, the size and frequency of those purchases and the likelihood that they will purchase a product again or recommend it to others. In his real-life business lab in Fredericton, Jim Gilbert learned that the real goal of branding is creating a biochemical bond.

Biochemically induced brand loyalty doesn't happen with pitch-driven ads born of logic and backed by data or limited-time offers: "Act now! Save money! Don't miss this one-time event!" As Dr. Zak explains, "The release of oxytocin shows that a story has created an emotional connection in any listener or viewer and this is why it provokes action."

Human minds think in pictures and stories. Every culture on the planet bathes its children in stories and images with nightly rituals of fables and fairy tales. Think about it: when was the last time you heard of a kid who went to bed at night, got tucked in and pleaded, "Mommy, could you please read me a statistic?"

Dollar Shave Club and Wheels & Deals have shown how it's possible to bypass larger competitors, leap tall buildings and stop speeding locomotives when you discover, tell and live your own story. Once you become true to who you already are, there isn't much the competition can do. From

Jim and Dawna's perspective, becoming Canada's Huggable Car Dealer was never a one-time promotional stunt, but
more of a poetic way to capture a timeless, emotional truth
already woven into their genetic makeup.

With the courage of their convictions and faith in themselves, the Gilberts created an irresistible brand simply by
standing in that truth, online and off.

Over the course of time, the Gilberts have built a brand
reputation some describe as being equivalent to the Apple,
Disney or Ferrari of its category. Inside their competitive
space of 243 other car dealers within 150 miles of their
location—or even those within the rest of the 3,426 miles
that connect Canada from east to west—there is nothing
quite like it. It's a one-of-a-kind original. What began with
a series of peculiar, counterintuitive radio ads eventually
morphed into a branding steamroller, overwhelming many
of the competitors in its path.

From a brain science point of view, the real magic of
storytelling is the long-term impact it has for any person or
enterprise once it starts to spread from one biochemically
activated human to another, and outward to other human
tribes who now gather around digital campfires and share
stories that matter to them.

What Exactly Is a B-R-A-N-D?

Never in a million years did we anticipate the type of wild
success generated by Canada's Huggable Car Dealer. Along
the way, however, some key principles emerged that guided

the overall strategy as we unpacked what we learned on our shared adventure.

It begins with a clear definition of the word B-R-A-N-D— specifically as it relates to fueling business results.

This powerful five-letter word is still one of the most misunderstood and misapplied terms in the entire business lexicon. Your brand is not your logo or visual identity stamp. This is not about making a graphic statement like the original definition related to cattle branding. Ask a hundred so-called marketing experts to define "brand," and you'll get about the same number of answers. As I searched for a more concrete way to define this abstract concept, I remember feeling like a miner during the California Gold Rush of 1849, striking it rich with a single sentence from author Karen Post in her 2004 book *Brain Tattoos*:

"A brand is a story embedded in the mind of the market."

It was like unearthing our own version of the Holy Grail.

This one single line in the third paragraph of the introduction to Post's book nailed it. The word "embedded" implies that stories have the power to deeply penetrate a person's psyche at a level far below the surface, like a permanent tattoo that inhabits the subconscious, subterranean world of the "mind." And the term "market" is today more fluid than ever, considering how any enterprise of any size now has the ability to instantly access a growing global audience of digital consumers and ambassadors.

Michel Dubin and Jim and Dawna Gilbert demonstrate that the real definition of "brand" has little or nothing to do with elements from a visual style guide, such as logos, fonts, colors, graphic design or trademarks. These are just visual representations of the story being told. It might help to think of the "brand," or the story, as a noun, and "branding" as a verb—like the tools and actions you use to tell and live that story.

That's the hardest part.

Living the brand. Living it each and every day, and with each customer and employee. With each online or community interaction.

More than anything, the narrative of Canada's Huggable Car Dealer became an internal, cultural North Star, establishing higher standards of service, teamwork and community spirit. Properly crafted, a compelling brand narrative acts like a powerful beacon to the outside world, and an endless source of energetic karma in how the brand is perceived and felt by people inside the organization. Jim and Dawna Gilbert are living proof that it's possible to shift public perception—no matter what category you compete in.

Like Da Vinci, Disney and Michael Dubin, the Gilberts know it's not enough to rely on great products or exceptional customer service. Those are just required elements. Common as table salt, they exist with every merchant on every street corner and every Amazon shipment. To be sure, no amount of marketing wizardry can compensate for a shabby, inferior product. However, legacy builders determined to win long term will recognize how the premium quality of their offerings can be augmented by taking a longer view towards Strategic Drama: projecting a brand story and personality that reflects the true essence of an organization.

But, it's never easy at first.

For us, it began with a 3,000-mile journey, deep into the heart of Texas.

The Branding Road Less Traveled

Without any promises or sureties, Jim Gilbert and I hopped on a flight and went searching for ways to sharpen our message. The idea itself was conceived at the world famous Wizard Academy, located outside of Austin, Texas, through Wizard of Ads partner Ray Seggern. Once he got to know Jim as a friendly, kind-hearted person and understood his values, Seggern developed the initial radio scripts and campaign that captured the personality of Canada's Huggable Car Dealer.

In other words, Seggern identified the poetic expression of real-life values and personality that were already there. When Jim woke up to the realization he was going to be called "Huggable," he began to experience plenty of reservations and sleepless nights.

"What will other people think?" he wondered. "Am I going to get laughed out of town? Am I risking everything Dawna and I worked so hard to build? Am I crazy... do I need to see a psychologist?"

But Jim's inner voice and conscience whispered that any successful business had to be about more than "four wheels and a piece of tin"—a metaphor he used to describe any competitor's offering that has no appreciable difference in quality, price, selection or service. From the day we met in 2002, "four wheels and a piece of tin" became a catchphrase to describe our quest to achieve substantial differentiation beyond the functional attributes of any product.

After pulling the trigger in September 2006 and the "Huggable" moniker making a splash on the airwaves, Jim was openly laughed at by many competitors at the weekly car auctions he would attend. Fellow dealers would poke fun, mock and make jokes at his expense, or, worse, ridicule him behind his back.

Through it all, Jim and Dawna stayed positive, because they put their trust in what real flesh-and-blood customers on the ground were saying. No matter how much their industry rivals chirped, the Gilberts kept smiling, hugging, being different, dreaming big and taking care of what mattered most: their employees, customers and community.

Over the ensuing years, Jim and Dawna have built playgrounds, supported local anti-bullying programs and nursing homes, sponsored youth athletic teams, created an online university and undertaken many other community initiatives. The Gilberts and their team differentiate by doing what they say. Living out their brand values of caring, kindness and originality in a manner consistent with what you would expect from "Canada's Huggable Car Dealer." The most powerful thing you can do for your business and brand is to become a real-life embodiment of the magical elixir of your own story.

It worked for Walt Disney when he began telling bankers and investors about the hollow-tree headquarters he planned for the Mickey Mouse Club. It worked for Michael Dubin when he channeled his love for sketch comedy into a YouTube blockbuster. It also turned out pretty good for Jim and Dawna Gilbert from the day they stepped into the moral authority of living their own story, surpassing many competitors in their region.

Timeless Takeaways

#1. It's not about "four wheels and a piece of tin."

Your products and services are not your brand. Neither is your logo. The success of any brand strategy hinges on the dramatic appeal of the compelling story you can legitimately represent in the mind of the market. Ultimately, that story becomes the position you aspire to occupy in the collective brain of humans.

The quality of your product or the merits of your service is not based on what you claim it to be. "Better" is only truly judged in the eye of the beholder. The discipline of brand strategy acknowledges that perception is reality. To be perfectly clear: there have been plenty of bad products in the history of consumerism, and no amount of clever storytelling can compensate for inferior goods or substandard service. But Jim and Dawna recognized that quality was table stakes—a starting point on their branding odyssey, not the final destination.

#2. Do you have the "moral authority" to tell your story?

Moral authority is the ability to influence people through the virtue of your character and deeds. That's why the brand story you tell must be true to you. It has to capture and encompass who you really are and how you conduct your daily business from the moment the sun comes up. You can't claim to be something you're not, or wear a marketing toupee. No one can put their faith and trust in a leader who says one thing and does another.

If Jim and Dawna had been anything less than kind-hearted or ethical, there is no way the "Huggable" story would have been believed or shared. Moral authority aligns vision, values and a consistent set of behaviors that inspire shared beliefs. Like legends of yesteryear—Amelia Earhart, Jackie Robinson, Rosa Parks, Terry Fox—this is the highest level of influence any leader can have.

#3. Strategic Drama demands raw courage.

The "Huggable" idea looks brilliant in hindsight, but the achievements enjoyed by Jim and Dawna came from a place of considerable emotional courage. Before they discovered who they really were—beyond their products—the Gilberts had to decide who they were *not*. They had to reject the traditional marketing practices of their category. Intellectually, anyone can understand that Strategic Drama means your company story is your brand strategy. But there is an emotional price to be paid by the leader whose job it is to discover, tell and, more importantly, live that story.

Any bold move to the thin outer reaches of a branch demands something more. Some gravel in your guts. Some spit in your eye. Steely resolve to stay on course with your commitment to long-form Strategic Drama—no matter what critics or opponents may say.

The Last Mile

Starting your own story engine requires any leader to embrace the wisdom of uncertainty. It entails trusting your instincts and following an unclear path to where intuition takes you.

Since those first radio ads launched in September 2006, the Gilberts's otherwise ordinary used car lot has served as metaphorical laboratory for anyone eager to examine the extraordinary connection between science, storytelling and human buying behavior. There may not be a precise, straight line of sales data that runs from teddy bears to the balance sheet, but Jim and Dawna know in their hearts that it's there.

There will always be others playing small, short-term games, willing to cut corners and forsake the future for today's sale. Someone else will pounce on opportunities to make a fast buck, run fake testimonials, fudge numbers or take kickbacks. But long-term leaders who operate with moral authority and understand the implications of creating Strategic Drama can turn time into an ally and build brands that are consistent with their vision, values, character and actions.

Pretending and posturing can be exhausting.

History and hard science reveal that storytelling is no fairy tale. Market evidence indicates that purposeful storytelling isn't just show business, it's good business.

When you know who you are—beyond your products and services—your competitors tend to fade in the rear-view mirror and become more irrelevant with each passing day.

Once you get your brand story straight, it has no expiry date.

You just need to know which story you want to start telling.

First, think. Second, dream.
Third, believe. And finally, dare.

WALT E. DISNEY

3

THE SEVEN PLOTS THICKEN

Four Fat Guys Discover Diamonds in the Desert

July 26, 2009

"Rick, you're never going to get a f**king TV show. All this is going to be is another week of bulls**t that we all have to go through."

This was not the first time Rick's dad had told him that having their own TV show was a dumb idea.

The conceptual seed was firmly planted in Rick's imagination in the early 2000s. PBS had aired a documentary about the family business in 2001. Several years later, a Los Angeles TV station featured the store as one of the "Ten Best Places to Shop in Las Vegas."

A self-described science and history bookworm, Rick openly wondered whether there was a TV show waiting to be discovered inside his family's strange and often surreal business. The more he thought about it, the more convinced he became that his otherwise ordinary business would benefit greatly from having its own show. No one else seemed to think so. His curmudgeon-like father—also his business partner—kept rejecting the idea out of hand, insisting it was a crazy pipe dream. Multiple production companies told him the same thing, asserting that "no one wants to see a TV program about four fat guys in a pawn shop." Rick persisted, however, stuck to his antique Civil War guns and eventually wound up in negotiations with HBO to shoot a pilot episode.

Hopes were high. A major network wanted to make Rick's dream a reality. As the Brazilian author Paulo Coelho penned in *The Alchemist*, "When you want something, all the universe conspires in helping you to achieve it."

If you're a guy like Rick searching for your own personal legend, you need to be prepared to fall down seven times and get up eight. True to form, Rick's initial plan didn't quite work out. HBO wanted to take the show in a seedier direction and portray the darker side of Vegas life—the tragic desperation of those who came to sell their belongings. But that wasn't the story Rick wanted to tell. He pictured something entirely different—something with humor, offbeat lessons from history, and plenty of room for the joy of discovery.

Then, a phone call came straight out of left field.

While in Las Vegas for a 2008 bachelor party, Brent Montgomery of Leftfield Pictures noticed the usually high number of pawn shops in the area. Thinking the sector might provide the backdrop for an interesting reality TV concept, Brent reached out to the Gold & Silver. Within a week, Brent and his Leftfield crew showed up to shoot the pilot. Three months later, on a Friday in February, they took their sizzle reel and pitched it to executives at the History Channel.

By Tuesday, they had a deal.

The rest, as they say, is history.

What History Channel bigwigs saw was exactly what Rick Harrison had pictured all along. A brighter, laugh-and-learn program focused on the historical merits of the unusual items and artifacts that customers brought to the store. Sprinkle in drama from face-to-face negotiations over the value of those precious objects and the generational dynamics and offbeat interplay between the four main characters in this family business and you ride an endless roller coaster of deals, steals, heroes and heels.

When *Pawn Stars* made its History Television debut in July 2009, Rick and his dad employed about a dozen people at their location on South Las Vegas Boulevard. For a few months after the first airing, customer traffic remained normal. Then, one day in December, Rick rubbed his eyes in disbelief. There was a line outside his shop of more people than he could count. His TV show was becoming a cult hit.

Soon, the crowds had mushroomed to the point where they needed to hire security to manage the crowd. Rick's business was experiencing the full-throttle benefits of the Mona Lisa Effect, to the point where people were queuing up well before the shop opened at 9 a.m. Sales skyrocketed. The number of employees quadrupled. Thanks to his conviction that his family business had a story worth sharing, Rick's wildest dreams were coming true.

If you were to ask him, Rick Harrison would likely tell you that there was no logic, rhyme or reason why millions had suddenly become fascinated with his second-hand store as opposed to the hundreds of others located in the same city—other than gut instinct. In hindsight, one can see how Rick had leveraged the power of Strategic Drama to trigger biochemical responses in large numbers of people.

What unfolded at the Gold & Silver also speaks to how crucial it is for any business or brand to tell the right story.

The one that best suits them, their values and the audience they want to connect with. The mega-hit *Pawn Stars* is a perfect illustration of the seven very different types of story any searcher will encounter on the magical journey to discovering an irresistible brand.

The Long and Dusty Road to Glory

Since the beginning of time, prophets and warriors have wandered into the desert in search of answers. Inherently dangerous, there is something about being in the middle of bone-dry, barren isolation that helps you discover ancient truths and wisdom that can make the most outrageous ideas and visions come to life. In *The Alchemist*, Coelho uses the forbidding expanse of the desert as the setting for the story of a Spanish shepherd boy named Santiago who makes a dangerous trek toward the Egyptian pyramids in search of his treasure.

Santiago's journey mirrors what dreamers like Rick have sought for centuries. It also reflects the evolution of a small rail town located in southern Nevada, on the edge of 25,000 desolate square miles known as the Mojave Desert. Rugged, unforgiving, inhospitable terrain. It's where the American Dream moseyed into a rustic saloon, shook hands with the Wild West and sat down to have a stiff drink and roll dice. When Las Vegas was first incorporated in 1905, few would have wagered that this dusty outpost would eventually bloom into the Entertainment Capital of the World.

A sparkling diamond in the desert, Las Vegas is most famous for the eight-mile neon oasis that is "The Strip." There's no shortage here of showstoppers, highlighted by the elegant dancing water fountains at the Bellagio, the Luxor Hotel's Great Sphinx and Pyramid, Caesars Palace, the new home of the NFL Raiders and a string of structures that mimic iconic global landmarks. From sunup to sundown, Vegas offers a dazzling parade of glittery spectacle. It's easy to find temptation on every street corner. A cornucopia of slots, blackjack, rolling dice, champagne on ice, dancin' girls, lounge acts, superstars, caviar, dry martinis and flashy Lamborghinis.

When Rick was 16, he and his two brothers were informed by their parents that they were moving from sunny San Diego to Sin City in search of a new dream. Their southern California real estate business was tanking in the face of rising interest rates and, with only $5,000 to their name, the Harrisons pulled up stakes and headed to the desert to start over. Rick's father was a 20-year Navy veteran, a hard-working hustler who saw opportunity in dealing gold coins and jewelry. In 1988, Rick and his dad joined forces to open their own pawn shop, getting the Gold & Silver off the ground with an initial investment of $10,000.

Rick's obsession with history and the art of deal-making proved to be a natural fit for the pawn industry, which dates back to ancient Greece, Rome and Mesopotamia. Today, more than 11,800 pawnbrokers across the U.S. serve more than 30 million Americans each year, with annual industry revenues reaching about $14.5 billion. In certain respects, the Gold & Silver is no different from many other nonde-script second-hand shops serving down-on-their-luck folks who've been forced to put their prized possessions on hock in return for quick cash. But, thanks to the powerful, mag-netic attraction of their story, there is no other second-hand store like it.

When our family first visited 713 South Las Vegas Bou-levard in March 2015, we were fully unprepared for the experience. We never expected to see three full-time employees just working the parking lot to keep the crowd and traffic organized. By 11:30 a.m., more than 200 peo-ple were lined up and waiting to get in, anxious to gaze at everything from rare Jimi Hendrix guitars to Japanese samu-rai swords, Egyptian mummies to Civil War rifles, Super Bowl rings to original paintings from Pablo Picasso and Sal-vador Dalí.

Personally, I wasn't a big fan of the TV show when we dropped by that first time, but Dana's 16-year-old son Josh really wanted to go. Obliging the curious teenager, off we went, spending an hour and a half examining the trove of artifacts, memorabilia and merchandise. Before leaving we purchased about $100 worth of branded souvenirs and grabbed a few selfies and photo ops.

Plenty of other people behaved the same way that day, standing in line to satiate the irresistible urge to wander through history and browse this fascinating collection of vintage wares. The Harrisons' shop attracts 4,000 to 5,000 customers a day. Celebrity visitors have included everyone from Bob Dylan, Steve Carell and Katie Couric to members of Bon Jovi, Def Leppard and Lynyrd Skynyrd.

From headliners to housewives and everyone in between, there is a sizeable audience eager to bask in the glory of the past at the home of *Pawn Stars*, the world-famous Gold & Silver.

The average pawnbroker attracts about 150 customers per day, but the Gold & Silver is anything but average. The Harrisons' store is a real-world demonstration of the Mona Lisa Effect. It's another rare, shining example of how any business, of any size, in any category—no matter how sketchy that category is perceived to be—can leverage the timeless power of story. Like DSC and Canada's Huggable Car Dealer, it's how any business separates itself from its competition, creates unrivaled customer demand and emerges as a Big Little Legend.

Could a centuries-old storytelling framework explain why audiences ravenously consume multiple seasons of *Pawn Stars*? While it's tempting to dismiss this unlikely success as a fluke, what if there is more involved than just a stroke of Vegas luck? What if the Harrisons' uncommon tale perfectly aligns with nearly four decades of research from an intrepid British journalist determined to uncover why we become fascinated by certain types of stories?

Exploring the Seven Wonders

In his epic 2004 bestseller *The Seven Basic Plots: Why We Tell Stories*, Christopher Booker painstakingly chronicles how and why humanity has always resonated with strikingly similar stories through the ages. Booker's monumental

736-page tome is like a literary North Star, a comprehensive guide devoted to the art of storytelling.

Drawing on a vast array of examples dating back to the Bible, Chaucer, Dickens and Hollywood, and exploring genres that range from romance to war movies and detective novels, Booker shows how storytelling has held up a uniquely revealing mirror to the psychological development of our species over the past 5,000 years. This seminal piece of work presents a timeless framework for any leader or marketing visionary who aspires to build an irresistible brand. It explains how Shakespeare, Seuss, Spielberg, Coelho, *Pawn Stars* and many others have exercised unlimited creative freedom within a historically accurate paradigm.

From a purely practical point of view, *The Seven Basic Plots* serves as a useful filter to determine whether what you are communicating has any degree of dramatic relevance. Does your message even have a chance to intrigue, catch on and stick with an audience? Does it possess the potential to release oxytocin and trigger a biochemical response? The legendary brands that manage this trick have all created a story that aligns with at least one of the seven timeless plots that Booker has traced throughout the history of human narratives.

Plot #1: Rags-to-Riches

Cinderella, *Cinderella Man*, *Aladdin*, the Rocky series, *Rudy*, *Slumdog Millionaire*, *The Pursuit of Happyness*, *Happy Gilmore* and *Bohemian Rhapsody* all feature generally virtuous but downtrodden heroes who achieve great success. Through their own hard work, sweat equity and resilient spirit, these upstart characters manage to rise above their station in life and achieve what they desire most.

This plot is also reflected in well-known brands such as Jack Daniel's, Johnnie Walker and Colonel Sanders; in the self-made empires of Oprah Winfrey, LeBron James and Gary Vaynerchuk; and, yes, in Michael Dubin's Dollar Shave Club.

Plot #2: Overcoming the Monster

The hero overcomes an evil and powerful creature/person/ entity that has exerted a wicked, destructive force over people or planet. There is a metaphorical dragon that needs to be slayed. Examples of this plot include David & Goliath, *Dracula*, *Jaws*, the Star Wars series, *Little Red Riding Hood*, *The Old Man and the Sea*, *The Shawshank Redemption*, *Braveheart*, *Saving Private Ryan*, *Erin Brockovich*, *Ford v Ferrari* or any of the James Bond, Batman or Spider-Man films.

Think of how many brands try to battle an imposing enemy: Tide wages war on dirt and Tylenol takes down headaches. Nike urges us to slay our own personal demons of apathy and laziness. Virgin positions itself as the people's underdog against corporate airlines like British Airways. When Apple was a challenger brand taking on mighty IBM, their disruptive "1984" commercial echoed dystopian themes advanced by George Orwell in the battle against "Big Brother."

Plot #3: Rebirth

A flawed character faces a reckoning that forces them to change their ways, re-discover their true self and help the people around them. Rebirth is especially powerful because we recognize our own lesser traits in the protagonist and find hope in their redemption and renewal. This plot is reflected in tales such as *A Christmas Carol, The Grinch, As Good as It Gets, The Ugly Duckling, The Lion King, Schindler's List, Moneyball* and *Jerry Maguire.*

As a brand, Red Bull promises to turn you into a new person by giving you metaphorical wings. Dove promotes self-acceptance with its Campaign for Real Beauty. The entire network lineup on HGTV is another great example of this plotline, demonstrating how properties and relationships experience renewal and inspiring audiences to see themselves in those home makeover stories.

Plot #4: The Quest

Like Santiago's journey to the Great Pyramids in *The Alchemist*, the Quest represents a goal or achievement you desperately need to attain. Often with loyal companions or a guide along for the ride, the hero overcomes obstacles and temptations to attain her wildest dreams. Examples include *The Da Vinci Code, Raiders of the Lost Ark*, the Lord of the Rings trilogy, *The Social Network* and *Miracle*. From the Holy Grail to a gold medal, this plot is focused on a heroic protagonist searching for a virtuous prize.

Brands reflecting similar quests include Patagonia, Lululemon, Harvard, Ferrari, the rock band U2, The Old Course at St Andrews, Tesla, TED Talks and TOMS Shoes. Whether they represent symbols of accomplishments, ideas worth spreading, achieving inner peace or making the world a better place, all of these brands are aligned with the essential spirt of the Quest.

Plot #5: Voyage & Return

A hero ventures off to an unfamiliar, sometimes magical place, meeting new characters and overcoming a series of trials before finding their way back home. New friendships and newfound wisdom are often discovered as the protagonist comes back a changed person.

Alice in Wonderland, *Back to the Future*, the Star Trek series, *Finding Nemo*, *Forrest Gump*, the Harry Potter books and movies, *City Slickers* and *The Wizard of Oz* are some of the most gripping Voyage & Return stories ever told.

Disney, Airbnb, American Girl, Harley-Davidson, Starbucks, the rock band KISS, World Wrestling Entertainment and *Pawn Stars* draw heavily on this theme—the ultimate in fantasy and escapism. The customer is magically transported to an alternative universe: think of the mild-mannered accountant who trades his spiffy suit for biker leather, ties on a bandana and jumps on a bad-ass Harley to find freedom on America's back roads.

Plot #6: Tragedy

Few have taken pen to parchment and scripted a tragedy like the Bard.

William Shakespeare mastered this art form. The central figure is undone by a critical character flaw or the cruelty of fate. Tragic masterpieces like *Macbeth*, *Hamlet*, *King Lear* and *Romeo and Juliet* are classic examples of a protagonist falling into a downward spiral. From the ancient Greeks and Romans through Sorkin and Söderberg, Tragedy explores the darker side of the human experience. Classics include

The Godfather, Bonnie and Clyde, The Picture of Dorian Gray, A Few Good Men, Thelma and Louise, Titanic, The Perfect Storm and *The Big Short*.

Admittedly, Tragedy is a harder story to tell unless it's key to the appeal of your business model. Tragedy has proven effective for non-profit organizations, or for public service campaigns that implore us to quit smoking, save animals, help the homeless or feed the hungry. The Salvation Army, the Red Cross, the SPCA and, again, Mothers Against Drunk Driving are great examples of brands that align with Tragedy as a fundamental plot.

Plot #7: Comedy

Characters tossed into hyperbolic states of comic confusion. Resolution only happens when the story has played out to its extreme. Misperceptions lead to complications, entanglements and farce. Mixups and hiccups are cleared up and the happy ending arrives. This plot is reflective of Bugs Bunny cartoons; *The Flintstones*; *Notting Hill*; *Planes, Trains and Automobiles*; *Saturday Night Live*; *The Hangover*; the Bridget Jones series; *Anchorman*; *Curb Your Enthusiasm*; *The Office* and all nine seasons of *Seinfeld*.

When done right, Comedy can be hugely effective and highly profitable. The Government Employees Insurance Company was founded in 1936, but it wasn't until August 26, 1999, that a TV ad featuring a charming gecko with a Cockney accent helped the world become acquainted with GEICO. Dos Equis made a shipload of money with the bearded, debonair "Most Interesting Man in the World." More recently, Aviation Gin has enjoyed enormous success by spoofing the entire spirits industry, revealing how distillers spend hours meditating before apologizing to the juniper berries.

Making Dollars and Sense

The real value to understanding these plots is recognizing the role they play for any brand to create consistency, longevity and equity. They establish the entire storytelling direction your brand will take, which is why Tragedy never felt right to Rick Harrison. He didn't feel comfortable with audiences watching human train wrecks in slow motion. When HBO proposed a program focused on the many meth addicts and struggling sex workers who appear in the middle of the night, Rick Harrison didn't feel this was the right story to get behind.

Alternatively, nostalgia is a form of escapism and very much a part of the *Pawn Stars* overarching plot as the historical significance of the items transport the audience to a different place in time. Intuitively, Rick Harrison knew Voyage & Return was a strategic direction that felt much better than the Tragedy proposed by HBO.

The Seven Basic Plots draws a certain amount of disdain from highbrow literary critics who say Booker's work is guilty of massive oversimplification. These archetypes, however, are incredibly valuable for legacy-minded leaders seeking to apply timeless and market-tested models in crafting a more compelling, drama-soaked story. It's how you anchor your brand strategy to a consistent, plot-driven direction. It's how your ideas get heard and remembered for generations.

From his disapproving father to the many networks who said "no thanks" when Rick Harrison pitched his TV show, many people failed to recognize the story gold sitting before their eyes. Booker's voluminous research allows you to see things differently: an explosive cocktail of multiple plotlines reverberating through one small family business. Essentially, *Pawn Stars* uses three of these seven major plots, all intertwined with each other.

Escapist, nostalgic elements of Voyage & Return are applied at the Gold & Silver as they turn back the clock through the pages of history. Toss in a mixture of Comedy focused on the Harrisons' dysfunctional interactions (with loveable Chumlee as the fall guy) and Overcoming the Monster moments that occurs in stare-down negotiations, and you have an explosive dramatic trifecta. And don't forget an undercurrent of Rags-to-Riches from the Harrisons' incredible migration from the California coast to the Nevada desert.

At a foundational level, many brands have Rags-to-Riches origin stories. Apple and Amazon, for example, were hatched in a garage before becoming trillion-dollar companies. Neither Steve Jobs nor Jeff Bezos ever missed an opportunity to share their tales of humble early beginnings— they were scrappy underdog Rockys engaging in combat with Apollo Creeds of Commerce like Xerox, IBM, Borders and Sears.

Rick Harrison was never going to find his treasure by focusing on quality of merchandise, low prices, fair return policies or friendly and knowledgeable staff. To alter back-alley perceptions of his industry and create a larger-than-life brand, Rick knew he had to showcase the compelling story already inside his company. Anyone can get lucky with 15 minutes of fame and a boost in short-term sales, but three generations of Harrisons have earned much more mileage out of a brand story built to stand the test of time and to trigger their own Mona Lisa Effect. When all things are equal—and even when they're not—the one with the best story always wins.

Timeless Takeaways

#1. Your story *is* your strategy.
Don't permit "story" to become a hackneyed buzzword relegated to the marketing department. Billionaire venture capitalist Ben Horowitz once explained, "The mistake people make is thinking the story is just about marketing. No, the story is the strategy." *Pawn Stars* demonstrates that a compelling brand story can be the engine that drives success, defines culture and powers innovation, while attracting partners, investors and lineups of customers.

Horowitz—who made himself a Silicon Valley legend by investing in Airbnb, Facebook and Twitter—knew that a company's CEO has to be the "keeper of the story" who always keeps it compelling, on message and up to date. But you don't need to be a famous VC to know that without Rick Harrison's leadership and storytelling the Gold & Silver would be just another pawn shop, like nearly 12,000 others in America.

#2. Find freedom within structure.

The Seven Basic Plots and its overarching themes are foundational for keeping your brand story both fresh and consistent. This framework can help guide your selection of metaphors, symbols, rituals and language for every form of creative expression, from words to photos, graphics, videos and more. Within at least one of these basic plots, or several blended together, you can create an original blueprint that will steer your brand strategy for decades.

Think of Canada's Huggable Car Dealer, which in many respects reflects elements of a romantic comedy like *Runaway Bride* fused with Disney-flavored elements of Voyage & Return. Or Michael Dubin of Dollar Shave Club, who took *Saturday Night Live*–style sketch comedy and sprinkled it with touches of Rags-to-Riches and Overcoming the Monster to illustrate the uphill battle consumers face against faceless, monolithic corporations.

#3. Build consistency, longevity and equity.

In addition to an array of superpowers, superheroes also come with many zeros. Combined gross revenues for the Batman, Spider-Man and James Bond franchises represent about $73.4 billion. The Mickey Mouse & Friends franchise has brought in about $70.5 billion while Harry Potter has done okay, with about $30.8 billion. Each of these legendary brands has intangible assets worth squillions of dollars. Each started their logic-defying ascent from a bank account of zero.

The integrity of an original idea, housed in a sturdy framework to tell multiple stories, establishes consistency and longevity while building public trust and financial equity. The brooding persona of Batman was first depicted in *Detective Comics* #33, published in November 1939. *Pawn Stars* first appeared on History Television on July 26, 2009, while Canada's Huggable Car Dealer launched with September 2006 radio ads and Dollar Shave Club made its debut in March 2012 on YouTube. Regardless of platform or media vehicle, Booker's *Seven Basic Plots* have proven to be an incredibly resilient framework, adaptable to changing times and technology while legacy brands continuously flourish and prosper.

Closing Credits

Chaos is the natural order of the universe.

Stories are one way we make sense of that chaos. Like many religions, irresistible brands develop traction through stories.

Since we first waited in line at the Gold & Silver in March 2015, it was readily apparent to Dana and me that much more than an assortment of rare and unusual merchandise was on display. It was storytelling in its finest and most exquisite form, supported by a wondrous, centuries-old composition that helps any business and brand connect with audiences well into the future. The real treasure of understanding *Pawn Stars* and how it relates to Booker's *Seven Basic Plots* is in seizing the opportunity to apply a sense of structure to the frenetic, blurry randomness of everyday life while helping audiences feel alive and connected. Weaving similar literary techniques knitted together by legendary wordsmiths like Shakespeare, Hemingway, Rowling and Coelho can elevate your brand as you simplify and hone your message to captivated audiences.

It's poetically fitting that *Pawn Stars* and its uncanny alignment with *The Seven Basic Plots* suddenly appeared in Las Vegas, a glittering spectacle that went from ghost town to gold mine. Standing alone on the periphery of the desert, Las Vegas is the ideal location for anyone who believes they can change their life story with one roll of the dice. The Mojave is also the perfect metaphor for dreamers and doers willing to wander arid deserts of apprehension and uncertainty to unearth personal truths and discover their destiny.

Big Little Legends recognize that reaching the oasis and setting yourself apart requires you to view and craft your business and brand with the eyes and soul of an artist. The biggest hurdle any leader encounters on this journey is the fear of failure and rejection, along with that nagging inner voice planting seeds of self-doubt. An unknown writer felt similar feelings before making a 1987 personal pilgrimage along 400 miles of an ancient trail in northern Spain.

He started wondering why so many of us abandon our dreams and become content to go through the mundane motions of daily life. His trek along the Camino de Santiago inspired a profoundly spiritual allegory about a shepherd boy in search of his treasure. Despite positive reviews, his original publisher opted not to reprint the book after its initial run of 900 copies. His dream had every reason to die right there.

Recovering from this setback, the writer and his wife left their Brazilian home and spent 40 days searching for answers in the Mojave Desert.

Upon his return, the nomadic writer continued the struggle. Kept knocking on doors. Refused to forsake his quest.

Eventually Paulo Coelho became the world's most translated living author. Together, *The Alchemist* and his 30-plus other books have sold in the hundreds of millions, published in more than 170 countries and translated into more than 80 languages.

Like Rick, Jim and Dawna, Michael and others you will meet in forthcoming chapters, Coelho's legacy character Santiago reveals how your quest will prompt the universe to begin speaking to you through many omens, signs and symbols.

You will stumble and sometimes fail along the way, but the key to discovering your personal legend is to never give up.

And to roam through real and metaphorical deserts long enough to come face-to-face with your own story.

The act of discovering who we are
will force us to accept that
we can go further than we think.

PAULO COELHO

PART II

BEING
DIFFERENT
BEATS BEING
BETTER

4

WORD-OF-MOUTH HEAVEN ON HIGHWAY 11

A Never-Ending Lineup in the Middle of Nowhere

May 28, 1968

About an hour north of Toronto, Highway 400 offers you the choice to either head to Sudbury or to North Bay.

Left or right. Either way, you're going way up north— deep into Canada's great outdoor wilderness. Skyscrapers, luxury high-rises and big-city traffic fade from your rear-view mirror.

Veer right, follow the North Bay route, and you'll turn on to Highway 11. Once you you're about five miles past Orillia, you'll bear witness to one of the most unbelievable, unlikely examples of a Big Little Legend to be found anywhere on the North American continent. Like many other drivers, your head will turn. You will be tempted to pull over to find a place to park. Before long, you'll be waiting in a lengthy but fast-moving line of fellow burger-craving travelers, and you'll experience the Mona Lisa Effect for yourself in one of the more remote parts of the small business world.

Welcome to Webers on Highway 11.

Referring to Webers as a "burger joint" is like saying the Louvre is a "building with a bunch of pretty pictures." Among Ontario cottage-goers, this roadside restaurant attraction and summer ritual has attained landmark status, with a word-of-mouth reputation that dwarfs any of its competitors.

But it wasn't always this way.

In the spring of 1968, the Beatles were recording their *White Album*, Muhammad Ali had been stripped of his world heavyweight boxing title after refusing to fight in Vietnam and Paul Weber Sr. was trying to figure out how to attract more customers. On the same day the Montreal Expos were awarded a franchise in baseball's National League, Paul was about to hit a marketing grand slam.

A father of six and a World War II airman who had survived a fiery crash in a Lancaster bomber, Paul had started his small company in the summer of '63. Within his first year of operation, he wound up losing about $3,000—a fortune back then. Undeterred, Paul picked himself up and hung in there. Around the time Sonny Liston hit the floor in '64 and lost the heavyweight crown to Cassius Clay, Paul's burger joint started to find its footing. Little by little, the eatery slowly grew popular with the cottage country crowd traveling north each summer to Lake Muskoka. From his days in the air force, the qualities of grit, tenacity and the ability to improvise were serving Paul well. On a daily basis, he learned to manage staff, solve cash flow issues, meet payroll and attract just enough customers to keep his fledgling burger operation up and running.

Then, one fateful day in May 1968, everything changed.

Paul had become friendly with a fellow veteran who worked for the Canadian National Railway. The two war buddies got to talking. Before long, a discontinued CN Rail caboose was being shipped north to Paul's location to sit on a set of train tracks laid next to the restaurant. They could use the caboose as a staff change room and a place to store kitchen and food supplies. Unknowingly, Paul had unleashed a thunderous left hook of marketing genius. The caboose was forcing drive-by motorists to take a second look.

The cost of doing something remarkable is dirt cheap compared to the bill for a status quo marketing plan that doesn't work.

It's no different today. If you don't do something remarkable, you won't offer anything worth talking about. Whether he was aware of it or not, Paul Weber Sr. had plugged into a time-honored concept proven to be a much safer bet than mindlessly pumping quarters into any number of marketing slot machines. With one bold move, Paul distanced himself from the competitors who were chasing instant results with short-term advertising. With that initial railway car, Webers began to experience organically generated word-of-mouth marketing: a highly potent commercial cocktail that companies can actually budget and plan for.

Starting with a single caboose, Paul discovered that being dramatically different beats the hell out of just being better. While everyone else in the burger category was focused on products, menu options and service, Paul headed in a completely new direction. With everyone else content to zig, Paul was performing a *zag*! The results of that May 1968 maneuver have been felt at the Webers' cash register and on the balance sheet for decades.

On an average day, Webers serves about 800 hamburgers an hour. Roughly 8,000 in a single day. They offer nearly a hundred picnic tables on wide green spaces, scattered around nine former CN railway cars, one of which serves as an indoor dining area. Celebrity sightings are frequent, with the likes of Goldie Hawn and Kurt Russell, Marie Osmond, Shania Twain, Martin Short, Masters champion Mike Weir, Alex Rodriguez, Frank Mahovlich, the Tragically Hip and the Barenaked Ladies being irresistibly drawn to drop by for a visit.

One man can still testify to the mouth-watering magic of the Webers legacy. A grill man with the original store in '63, Mike McParland is the only remaining link to Webers' storied past. Beginning when he was 16 years old, Mike has been flipping hamburgers for 58 consecutive years under three different owners. Now retired after more than 35 years of teaching and refereeing basketball, Mike vividly remembers what it was like when Paul Weber Sr. first set up shop. "Before Mr. Weber bought the place, it was an old fruit stand, just struggling to stay alive. I was still in high school when I started working for Mr. Weber and listening to him say, 'Keep it simple, Sally.' Don't overcomplicate things, keep a tight rein on the menu items. And keep the place tidy. If you have to time to lean, you have time to clean."

In 1989, Paul Sr. turned the business over to Paul Jr.; in 2004, the company was sold to Guelph, Ontario, businessman Tom Rennie. Coincidentally, both Rennie and McParland are graduates of Western University in London, Ontario—where they don't teach a whole lot about building legendary brands through the power of word-of-mouth marketing.

What You *Won't* Learn in an MBA Program

The halls of academia are a wonderful venue for learning business theory, wrapped in proper protocols and standardized grammar.

Universities are intellectual fountains of precise terminology, correct buzzwords, sophisticated enterprise models and mental constructs designed to make people look and feel intelligent in corporate boardrooms. Academic-based language supported by copious numbers of case studies, validated by empirical analysis, white papers and written exams. There is no better vehicle than a high-level MBA program to flood you with data-focused market research, conjoint analysis, behavioral economics, Bayesian statistics and the impact of non-standard decision-making in commercial markets using evolutionary game theory.

Graduates of these institutions often wind up occupying high-level corporate positions and become well versed in the art of business-speak (often in the form of pretentious gibberish with a focus on mission-critical objectives designed to influence early adopters within available bandwidth and core competencies that promise first-mover advantage). Neat and tidy economic models can't explain how the ratio between brilliant ideas and pure bulls**t often lands on the wrong side of the ledger.

Linear-based logic and mathematical rationality is perfect for someone responsible for building locomotives or keeping the trains on time. It is, however, woefully inadequate when dissecting a three-word description of the most cost-effective and productive form of long-term marketing and brand building the world has ever known.

Word-of-mouth.

The numbers are beyond staggering:

- 92% of consumers trust recommendations from friends.

- W-O-M generates 5x more sales than paid media.

- 88% of customers trust online reviews.

- Brands that create an emotional connection with their customers receive 3x more W-O-M than those that don't.

Business schools don't tend to offer proven curriculum designed to teach the enigmatic mystery of creating word-of-mouth magic. If not for the Webers of the world, where else would you learn and apply this level of sorcery that has worked for decades?

Some marketing experts believe positive word-of-mouth and its inherent capacity to multiply has the potential to generate 30% to 60% growth in a given fiscal year, depending on the industry. As Harvard business professor Fred Reichheld wrote, "The value of any one customer does not reside only in what that person buys. It's what they are prepared to tell others about you that can influence your revenues and profits just as much."

Despite this effectiveness, a recent report from the American Marketing Association found that while 64% of executives believe word-of-mouth is the most powerful form of marketing, only 6% feel they've mastered it. Educated suits and ivory tower academics know this stuff is important. Doing it and achieving measurable, real-world results is another matter altogether.

Unlike high-level strategy, finance or product innovation, marketing involves a direct connection with actual customers. Online or off—marketing is connected to those who show up with cash and credit cards, as well as to the other real folks who stay away, ignore you or buy from somebody else. Real customers with their many moods and opinions do not converse in the language of business-speak. They don't see the world through year-end reports, slide decks, flow-charts, strategy documents, bullet points or spreadsheets.

Flesh-and-blood humans who become loyal customers are wonderfully chaotic, unpredictable and fickle creatures, filled with biases, quirks, emotions and idiosyncrasies. Volcanic word-of-mouth only erupts when people with a pulse can experience something far outside their daily norms and existence.

> Wow... well, would you lookie over there at that, Martha! Let's pull over and see what that caboose is all about. Wonder where they got it? How would you ever get the damn thing shipped up here?

No one—including you—has ever taken pains to tell a friend about an average or adequate restaurant visit. Slightly exceeding expectations with a 10% off coupon or a "7th Coffee Is Free!" card won't crack the word-of-mouth coconut. No heads will turn.

When thousands of weekly travelers on Highway 11 started seeing an honest-to-goodness authentic caboose sitting next to a burger stand, they saw something completely *different*. This pattern began to repeat itself daily and then a thousand times over, week after week. And once the queue started forming on a consistent basis, that caused even more inquisitive, drive-by rubberneckers to stop and see what the fuss was all about. And then those customers started telling others about the unique burger joint on Highway 11.

> You can't miss it, Fred... it's the one with the caboose beside it.

One of the surest ways to trigger a word-of-mouth chain reaction is to invest in a Physical Icon: a landmark structure or piece of architecture that stands out like a hot pink leprechaun wearing purple polka-dot shoes. Multiple studies on the subject of spatial cognition from institutions such as the University of Melbourne and the University of Pennsylvania have confirmed that human subjects are naturally wired to use physical landmarks as a form of mental shorthand for both memory and navigation. A Physical Icon activates the hippocampus area of our brain, helping orient us while attaching meaning and context to those objects.

Think of it as the equivalent to having a GPS in your brain that triggers natural homing and recognition instincts. From a long-term brand-building perspective, any increase in human recognition tends to accelerate the potential for attracting attention, deeper emotional connection and, eventually, consumer selection.

From the Eiffel Tower to the CN Tower and the Leaning Tower of Pisa, plenty of Physical Icons have demonstrated their ability to exert mystical, magnetic powers that persuade real humans to willingly surrender precious time and attention. For centuries, people have been attracted to man-made structures such as the Great Pyramids or the Great Wall of China, or to natural wonders like Niagara Falls and the Matterhorn. Similar spatial cognition elements are inherent in the Statue of Liberty, the "Rocky" statue in Philadelphia or the world's tallest moose statue in Moose Jaw, Saskatchewan. Noteworthy Physical Icons include the lighthouse at Peggy's Cove, Nova Scotia; the Taj Mahal in Agra, India; the giant nickel in Sudbury, Ontario; the Bavarian-themed downtown of Frankenmuth, Michigan; Christ the Redeemer in Rio, Brazil; the famous River Walk in San Antonio, Texas; and the imposing, 55-foot Jolly Green Giant in Blue Earth, Minnesota.

When Steve Jobs wanted to establish a flagship store to anchor Apple's retail network, he ordered the construction of a 32-by-32-foot glass cube edifice on New York's busy Fifth Avenue. When the doors opened in May 2006, it quickly became one of New York's most photographed landmarks. Opening-day celebrity star power included Kevin Bacon, Beyoncé, Kanye West, Spike Lee and Dave Chappelle, who all helped generate more word-of-mouth buzz that eventually attracted more than 18 million people in its first year of operation.

Physical Icons encompass any truly interesting—even unrelated—object that draws attention. McDonald's erected a Physical Icon in the early 1970s when they first put up a playground next to their restaurant in Chula Vista, California. Business spiked by 34% before the park was even completed, generating a 63% hike in volume over subsequent months. Red Bull created buzz by perching a giant beverage can on top of a Mini Cooper. In November 2019, Starbucks opened the world's largest coffee shop on Chicago's "Magnificent Mile": a five-story, 35,000-square-foot java-inspired theme park. Complete with curved escalator encircling a 56-foot coffee-bean cask, this state-of-the art emporium has attracted hordes of eager customers, all willing to stand in line to immerse themselves in the Starbucks Reserve Roastery experience. Physical Icons also dot the landscape at Canada's Huggable Car Dealer, with the kiddies' merry-go-round and a well-appointed nature walk that surrounds the property known as the "Trail of Hugs."

Science and history repeatedly confirm that creating a Physical Icon is one of the three best investments a leader can make to establish a permanent force that grabs attention and triggers a word-of-mouth following. But what happens when your best-laid plans are thrown asunder by events beyond your control?

How does any leader react when their business ship gets torpedoed in broad daylight?

A Footbridge to Fortune

When customer traffic picked up in the late 1960s and mushroomed through the '70s, Webers suddenly had a new problem to deal with. The restaurant had become such a hit that hungry homebound travelers who stopped on the opposite side of Highway 11 were risking injury or death by running across the road, dodging traffic while holding babies—just to get a taste of those delicious char-broiled burgers. Evidently these were burgers worth dying for.

By the early '80s, the Ontario government saw a safety issue and stepped in. They built a concrete median to protect people from themselves. The barrier's impact on Webers' business was immediate. Sales dropped by 50%. It was as if someone had turned off one side of the customer tap—which, in effect, is exactly what happened.

Something had to be done. Something drastic. The Weber family couldn't just wave the white flag of surrender.

Searching for answers, Paul Jr. discovered a footbridge for sale in Toronto: it once connected the CN Tower to the other side of Front Street. He and his dad bought the bridge for $250,000 and had it installed over Highway 11. It was a risky move when you consider that interest rates at the time were about 22%. There were no guarantees this big-time investment would pay off. Paul Sr. worried it was far too much debt for his little burger place.

It was the biggest decision in company history. It wasn't about a new marketing approach. This was a matter of survival.

Looking back, current owner Tom Rennie questions whether the business would be where it is today had the Webers not exhibited that rare combination of vision and courage. "At a time when financing was very expensive, there was enormous risk involved as to whether people heading south would actually make the physical effort to pull over, cross the bridge and wait in line," Tom says. "But taking a chance is what any business owner needs to do when unexpected hurdles present themselves from competitors, the market or, in this case, from the Ontario Ministry of Transportation."

By October 1983, the newly refurbished, bright orange footbridge was firmly in place, along with a large parking lot on the southbound side of Highway 11. The pedestrian bridge put an end to reckless jaywalking while protecting southbound burger-maniacs from themselves. It remains the first and only privately owned footbridge over a public highway in the entire province of Ontario.

By next summer, sales at Webers skyrocketed by 60%.

The Webers' decision to gamble a quarter of a million dollars on its newest Physical Icon sparked decades of conversation among road-tripping Ontarians.

Did you hear about that new bridge Webers put up over Highway 11? Seems like people were running across the road and risking life and limb for those burgers. You gotta hand it to 'em, they think of everything. A trip up north ain't the same without stopping at Webers.

Game-changing word-of-mouth will never be generated by a company that delivers "exceptional customer service" or "a high-quality product." Those are expectations. Great service and top-notch products can boost retention and produce lots of positive feedback, but they aren't the foundation for a long-term word-of-mouth strategy that an organization can budget and pay for.

Tom Rennie freely admits the actual quality of the burgers, the freshness of the ingredients or the patties that are 100% Canadian beef don't register as being different enough to warrant a second look. They don't explain the long lineups. Any one of 99 other competitors could make an identical "quality-based" argument. Quality is assumed.

Every airline offers frequent-flying programs. Every detergent has special enzymes that make clothes "cleaner, whiter, brighter." Every financial planner offers a free, no-obligation consultation. Every major fast-food outlet has drive-thru service.

Original, unmistakable Physical Icons are not so easily duplicated.

It makes perfect business sense when you grasp the bottom-line impact of word-of-mouth marketing and the endless chain of referrals it generates. Generally speaking, it will cost a company five to ten times more to acquire a new customer than keep a current one. Meanwhile, Bain & Company estimates that even a 5% increase in customer retention can boost a company's profitability by 75%. Numbers, however, only tell part of the story for Tom Rennie.

A native of Guelph, Ontario, Tom grew up going to Webers, which was halfway between his family home and cottage—today, he still remembers listening to "Hard Day's Night" on the car radio as they headed north. A former college football player with the Western University Mustangs, Tom absorbed life-long lessons about teamwork, discipline and time management that would prepare him for his legacy career. While scouting for a new opportunity in 2003, Tom heard from a buddy that Webers might be for sale. As it turns out, the thought of becoming chief steward for an Ontario landmark was too tempting to resist.

Following his father's retirement in 1989, Paul Jr. had taken the helm and, on March 1, 2004, he sold the legendary burger emporium and handed the keys to the kingdom over to Tom Rennie, the loyal customer who had been stopping by since he was a kid.

One of the first staffers to introduce himself to Tom was original burger-flipper Mike McParland, who quickly grew to love how the new boss "thought big" to keep the Webers legend alive. His most recent initiative is a fully lit skating rink with ten-inch boards that gives locals and visitors something fun to do over the winter. The facility is free to use, and Mike says the ice surface is NHL-sized because "Tom likes to go big or go home." Besides building the rink, Tom also secured a Starbucks franchise for the property and purchased additional land on both sides of the highway for future legacy-enhancing projects.

When Mike first stepped behind the grill in the Webers burger ring, Sonny Liston was preparing to dethrone Floyd Patterson as world heavyweight boxing champion. Since then, no fewer than 81 champions have been crowned by four different governing bodies—including Muhammad Ali, Joe Frazier, George Foreman, Mike Tyson, Evander Holyfield and Lennox Lewis. Still standing in tip-top shape, Mike looks forward to being back behind the grill for a 59th consecutive summer of serving burgers. He confesses that when he married Margie, they had to honeymoon nearby so he could step back into the kitchen ring within a week. The McParlands have five children, and they all worked at Webers. When Mike and Margie's 16-year-old son Josh perished in a tragic van crash, Paul Jr. set up a memorial in the

Webers picnic area, where mom and dad still find comfort to this day.

Timeless Takeaways

#1. How will your customer do the marketing for you?

What needs to occur before any customer will whip out their phone, snap a selfie with your business in the background and do the marketing on your behalf? Without a clearly identifiable *zag*, it's impossible to expect that type of behavior to spread from one human to another. Before the advent of social media, brands spoke for themselves. A McDonald's billboard was bought and paid for by the corporation. Today, a social media post about Mickey D's originates from anyone with a phone or an internet connection.

With every customer tweet, Instagram or Facebook post, Webers on Highway 11 is plugging into the power of organic advocacy. Each day, hundreds of unofficial brand ambassadors tell and re-tell their story. Photo ops in front of vintage railway cars go a long way toward building brand equity many years down the line. Webers has created and nurtured an environment where ordinary people can share their extraordinary story. Erecting a Physical Icon is a way to inspire those brand ambassadors: the ultimate, zero-cost evergreen marketing strategy, one that's credible, reliable and cost-effective.

#2. Step up and cross your own footbridge to fortune.

Creating a word-of-mouth marketing frenzy is far from easy. Are you willing to explore what others won't and find a *zag* worthy of attention? You'll likely face obstacles beyond your control as you construct your own metaphorical footbridge— and need to overcome them.

Taking calculated risks comes with the territory for any leader who recognizes that grit and gut instincts can be more reliable than mathematical calculations. Otherwise, you're going to remain immobile, doing nothing more than what your competitors are doing. Thousands of small businesses have come and gone on Highway 11 since Paul Weber Sr. first set up shop in 1963. Each one was faced with many seemingly insurmountable hurdles, challenges and barriers. Each also had plenty of opportunities to be courageous, defy the odds, go against the grain and try new things. Leaders in any crowded marketplace have to recognize that fitting in can be fatal. A strategic decision not to stand apart represents a choice to remain invisible.

#3. Stewardship breeds successful entrepreneurship.

Tom Rennie sees himself as a custodian. A caretaker for a legend. He feels the responsibility for instilling a shared mission among his people to leave the place in better shape than they found it.

Stewardship is taking care of something that belongs to another. To this day, Tom considers it his job to maintain and keep building on what Paul Sr. started, and lead a cohesive team of which each member is proud to say they are a Webers employee. Turnover rates are low, primarily because of the shared sense of history for what they have established

on Highway 11 and how the business and brand continue
to evolve.

One Last Bite

In the summer of 2015, when Dana and I ventured north
on Highway 11 to visit family in Huntsville, there was no
question we were making the Webers pit stop. The first
impression was powerful. Despite the huge lineup, there
was systematic efficiency that would make Henry Ford or
Ray Kroc smile up in productivity heaven. The line moved
quickly that day, which happened to coincide with the 46th
anniversary of the Apollo 11 moon landing, when Neil Armstrong declared, "One small step for man, one giant leap for
mankind."

Similar to NASA astronauts exploring unknown frontiers,
Paul Weber Sr. had no guarantee that installing antique
railway cars or a pricey footbridge would generate word-
of-mouth magic in the midst of rocky, unpredictable and
uncertain times. Big Little Legends like Webers demonstrate that the difference between success and failure is not
necessarily better abilities or ideas, but the courage to trust
one's instincts. From its inception, Webers was always more
than just another hamburger stand on a lonely stretch of
highway. The specific reasons why Webers created a Mona
Lisa Effect in the middle of nowhere are no mystery. Not
when you understand the science that supports the permanent allure of multiple Physical Icons coupled with a
recurring tale from one of *The Seven Basic Plots*: in this case,
elements of Voyage & Return as customers escape into an

alternate universe fueled by nostalgia for simpler times and happy childhoods.

Toss in a workplace culture that oozes a "can-do" spirit since the year the Fab Four first unleashed Beatlemania along with a leader determined to create legacy and it adds up to a powerful recipe for long-term success. Through seven decades, Webers has demonstrated that building a Big Little Legend involves much more than just serving tasty burgers with great service at affordable prices. While many business owners, corporate executives and well-schooled marketers claim differentiation is a priority, few take pragmatic, concrete steps to make that type of *zag* happen.

Practical methods on generating word-of-mouth traffic aren't typically taught by scholarly snooty-snoots at reputable business schools. You don't need to be an academic brainiac or corporate titan to know that legends are never created by blending in with the crowd or playing a safe, risk-free hand.

How far will you go to clearly differentiate your brand from all the other folks selling the equivalent to burgers, shakes and fries in your category? What will you implement to get noticed, to get people talking and start spreading your story?

What makes you different makes you an original. What makes you original makes you a leader.

Whether you laid the initial tracks or took over the daily running of the train, stewardship is the highest level of leadership.

It's about being willing to lace up the gloves. Stepping into the ring and fighting for something larger than yourself.

Doing whatever it takes to keep your business and brand alive.

No matter what's standing in your way.

*Everyone has a plan until
they get punched in the mouth.*

MIKE TYSON

5

BUSINESS BOOMS WHEN FISH CAN FLY

Catch the Energy from Seattle to Savannah!

April 1, 1986

Think of iconic landmarks in the state of Washington, and what immediately comes to mind might be majestic Mount Rainier or Seattle's Space Needle. Then there's the Museum of Pop Culture, the Amazon Spheres, the Jimi Hendrix Memorial and a small, commodity-based business located on the Elliott Bay waterfront.

Back in 1965, however, the idea of including that small business in this discussion was as unlikely as putting a man on the moon and bringing him back to earth.

Three years after JFK shared the vision and four years before Neil Armstrong took that giant leap, John decided to take a big step of his own. One of several employees at a quiet little fish stand, John Yokoyama was trying to make ends meet and keep up with the monthly $150 payments on his brand-new '65 Buick Riviera. When his employer announced his upcoming retirement, John opted to take a chance and buy the company. He figured making those hefty car payments would be a lot easier on an owner's salary.

John was about to get experienced.

Almost overnight, he learned the hard way that just because you know how to work *in* a business doesn't mean you know how to *own* the business. For many years, his modest enterprise struggled. Just making payroll was a constant issue. Unknown outside of Seattle's downtown core, John's open-air stall wasn't much different from his many competitors, offering similar products at similar price points with similar levels of customer service.

He was also becoming somewhat of a crabby pants.

"For a long time, I was an angry manager, an angry owner," John says. "Days were long. The work was hard. No one was having any fun. All the tools in my managerial tool kit were fear-based." John gave his employees rules to follow based on "that's how we've always done it here." No one had permission to perform. Beyond frustrated and teetering on the edge of bankruptcy, John sat down with a business coach to brainstorm ways to save his sinking ship.

In one of those April 1986 coaching sessions, an employee suggested they try to become "world famous!" One idea led to another, and that's when John and his team committed to becoming something outrageously bigger and more meaningful than just fish sellers—something out of this world. Some would call it a "moonshot." Others thought they were bat-s**t crazy.

In effect, John gave everyone permission to bring their best selves to work each day. To stop treating work as though it was work. If his fish market was going to be famous beyond Puget Sound, then work itself was going to have to become a heck of a lot more fun.

Fish began to fly. Business started taking off.

Outside of John and his handful of employees, few would have wagered there would be a day when people from all over the world would flock to watch salmon and trout wildly tossed back and forth. Few could have foreseen a day when customers would fall in love with this brand of crazy—hook, line and sinker.

Since that fateful coaching session, John's otherwise ordinary, 800-square-foot shop has become recognized all over the planet as the "World Famous Pike Place Fish Market." The hilarious, goofy antics of John's fish-flinging workers have been featured on CNN, *The NFL Today*, MTV's *The Real World* and ABC's *Good Morning America*, among others. More than 10,000 weekly visitors stop by to enjoy the boisterous spirit and wacky merriment exhibited by Seattle's unofficial ambassadors. The Mona Lisa Effect occurs daily at a venue that is cold, wet and smelly, starring performers who wear orange aprons and rubber boots.

The workplace culture created by the Pike Place fishmongers has been captured on film and immortalized in print, and now attracts scores of celebrities and high-profile athletes to mug for the cameras. It even inspired the world's top-selling corporate training video series of all time. Remembering their early skeptics, John and his team know they've had the last laugh multiple times over. There's nothing silly about their daily pranks and shenanigans when it comes to the serious business of attracting enthusiastic customers and top talent. From their waterfront kiosk, the cod-throwing crowd-pleasers at Pike Place generate revenues in excess of $10 million a year. By creating and living their own story daily, Pike Place became the little fish market that could. Their retail profit margin per square foot ranks among the highest in North America.

Seeing Is Believing

My first encounter with these entertainers from the Emerald City was through their wildly popular FISH! videos—the 1998 training series that reveals four core principles of creating a highly engaging workplace. But a second visit in 2016 made something else glaringly obvious—something that didn't register previously. No longer fixated on the clownish capers and call-and-response tomfoolery of the Pike Place team, my focus shifted instead to the visible reactions of more than a hundred bystanders, jammed and crammed together like sardines. Plain to see. Swarms of humanity going bananas over fish!

Swept away by sketch comedy play-acting, the audience members were willing accomplices in this performance, straining to get a closer look at how a 40-pound chinook salmon is expertly heaved, caught and wrapped. Every now and then, an excited spectator would hop behind the counter to become part of the shenanigans. There were wide-eyed smiles and continuous laughter—but there were also dozens capturing the good-natured silliness in photos and videos on their phones. The new truth about creating the Mona Lisa Effect in our attention economy was speaking loud and clear.

What if any company could initiate its own chain reaction of energy where happy customers pull in more happy customers?

Pike Place Fish Market never relied on traditional marketing methods such as newspaper, TV or radio ads to spread their message. For years, those initial training videos not only got people talking, they also generated tons of free publicity that built this Big Little Legend to the point where first-time visitors to Seattle were dying to go and witness the magic for themselves. But with the power of mass media now in the hands of anyone with a mobile phone, it has become crystal clear how much the marketing game has changed.

Forever.

That same shift is making a man named Jesse jump for sheer joy in a sleepy Georgia town famous for its antebellum hospitality.

Jesse Cole and his wife Emily had no idea what they were getting into upon their 2015 arrival in Savannah. On their first visit to historic Grayson Stadium, the couple saw nothing but cloudy skies and empty seats. It was the same ballpark where Babe Ruth, Lou Gehrig, Hank Aaron and other legends once played, but for the most part professional baseball had been a failing enterprise in Savannah for almost a hundred years. After the New York Mets minor-league team pulled up stakes, the enterprising Coles thought there might be an opportunity for college summer baseball.

But first, they needed to change the atmosphere.

Starting with only two season-ticket holders, Jesse and Emily flipped the entire baseball experience upside down with a carnival-like approach that turned heads and attracted attention. The Savannah Bananas quickly made a name for themselves with offbeat, crazy promotions like Underwear Appreciation Night, with Jesse tossing "Dolce & Banana" undergarments into the crowd, and a 65-and-over senior citizen dance team called the Banana Nanas. Often compared to a latter-day P.T. Barnum, Jesse himself can be seen wearing a yellow tuxedo and top hat seven days a week, serving as the Bananas' ringmaster on and off the field.

Every aspect of the Bananas fan experience, online or off, is designed with energy in mind. Between innings, players do choreographed dances in front of the dugout. Once in a while they take to the field in kilts. The third-base coach wears cowboy boots. There are conga lines through the stands. There's a giant banana mascot named Split, a 30-member pep band and a first-base coach who specializes in breakdancing. The P.A. announcer mixes walk-up music with Hollywood movie clips. There are call-and-response theatrics with the Grayson Stadium faithful.

No wonder the Bananas are the hottest ticket in town: a destination for fans to enjoy good clean fun and share it with their friends on social media. Major television networks including ESPN, CNN and ABC have covered the Bananas and, prior to the COVID-19 crisis of 2020, they had generated 88 consecutive sellout crowds. But when you step back and analyze the overall brand strategy, it's astonishingly simple: provide competitive baseball that injects oomph and umph into the many dead spaces resting within America's pastime.

"From the get-go, our whole mindset is: whatever is normal, try to do the exact opposite," Jesse explains. "I think our starting point with everything is, 'What is the big problem?' For many people, the problem with baseball is that it tends to be long, slow and boring. In Savannah, essentially baseball failed for 90 years. We looked at the entire problem differently and asked, 'How do we create a circus where a baseball game breaks out?'"

Customers will do your marketing and build your brand for you, but only if you give them something remarkable, something worthy of sharing with friends, family and neighbors.

In Northern Ontario, Webers on Highway 11 struck a mighty power chord with the public by installing Physical Icons. But there are two other ways to inspire word-of-mouth magic and ignite the Mona Lisa Effect. In the case of the Savannah Bananas and Pike Place Fish Market, the specific recipe for attracting a pumped-up audience hinges on supplying an Energy Booster. Like applying a pair of jumper cables to the human heart, a high-voltage sensory jolt awakens us from routine and habitual behaviors. An Energy Booster is any form of activity, motion or commotion that interrupts normal patterns of predictable or customary experiences—shopping, dining, sightseeing, attending rock concerts. In many respects, Pike Place Fish Market and the Savannah Bananas borrow performance scripts straight out of early vaudeville, employing slapstick Comedy from *The Seven Basic Plots* while providing an escapist Voyage & Return experience.

Energy Boosters are packaged and presented in many different forms. In St. John's, Newfoundland, there is a time-honored ritual that occurs at watering holes on historic George Street. According to legend, this "screeching-in" ceremony began in World War II as a way to honor American soldiers who stopped by before heading off to Europe. Today, first-time visitors to the Rock are welcomed with an Energy Booster every time they get screeched in at a downtown pub. Newcomers take a shot of vile rum, a bite of Newfie steak (fried bologna) and kiss the head of a codfish before reciting: "Long may your big jib draw." The ceremony concludes with the grateful inductee awarded an official certificate as an honorary Newfoundlander, inspiring cheers from other patrons.

At Jim Gilbert's used car dealership, an Energy Booster is as simple as a friendly hug from a staff member. In Burlington, Vermont, Small Dog Electronics looks like any other tech retailer until you walk in and experience the shift created by the many employees who bring their dogs to work each day. Red Bull, the undisputed global leader for energy drinks, has generated buzz around live events like Crashed Ice (now known as the Ice Cross World Championship), reinforcing a strong brand image synonymous with adventure, thrill and adrenaline.

In the summer of 2014, the Ice Bucket Challenge in support of ALS went viral and raised over $220 million. Everyone from celebrities to politicians to ordinary people posted videos and shared that energy and awareness for the cause all over the internet. Beginning with a 2006 experiment involving a box of matchsticks, a Utah-based inventor used online video to share enthusiasm and energy for his high-performance blenders. The incredibly successful "Will It Blend?" campaign from Tom Dickson and Blendtec has destroyed iPhones, skis, marbles, explosives, foam footballs and more while racking up more than 290 million YouTube views entering 2021.

Large conferences featuring motivational speakers represent a different style of Energy Booster. In the arena of experiential learning, you would be hard-pressed to find anything like the high-octane culture-building program out of London, Ontario, known as The Pit Crew Challenge, an experience purposefully designed to shift mindsets and accelerate teamwork. Described as a rip-roaring adrenaline rush, the event—designed by Bob Parker—features a real-life NASCAR vehicle making a thunderous entry into a simulated pit area to help corporate clients learn, with hearts racing, how high-performance cultures are created.

Few performers in rock music ever created a word-of-mouth Energy Booster to rival the one displayed by a 24-year-old left-handed guitarist on June 18, 1967. As a supporting act at the legendary Monterey Pop Festival in California, Jimi Hendrix was a last-minute addition on a bill that included Jefferson Airplane, Janis Joplin, The Who and The Grateful Dead. A former army paratrooper, Hendrix wanted to make a name for himself as he prepared to make his debut appearance at the festival. Not be outdone by Pete Townshend and his guitar-smashing antics, Hendrix knew he had to kick it up a notch.

Legend has it that the Fender Strat Hendrix was supposed to play was switched up with a cheap imitation moments before he grabbed a 99 cent can of Ronsonol lighter fluid, soaked his guitar and set it ablaze following a blistering rendition of "Wild Thing."

Jaws dropped. No one in the audience had ever seen anything like it. That singular moment sparked a word-of-mouth wildfire, thanks to the iconic photo of the guitarist that landed on the cover of *Rolling Stone* magazine: Hendrix kneeling over his fiery axe with burning desire. By the time he headlined the original Woodstock Festival in

1969, Seattle's Jimi Hendrix was the world's highest-paid performer.

The Purple Haze of Differentiation

He may not have torched a Fender in front of 50,000 crazed rock fans, but once upon a time a bespectacled New York author delivered the literary equivalent. Seth Godin's diminutive, odd-looking book, published in 2003, forever changed the way we look at marketing.

It was called *Purple Cow*.

The little book with the unusual title was written for those who believed that marketing had become less effective because of clutter, more clutter, advertising avoidance and shrinking attention spans. *Purple Cow* was a manifesto that encouraged companies and their leaders to transform their businesses by being remarkable. Godin challenged leaders to produce unbelievably, undeniably extraordinary products and services for specific groups of customers, allowing them to bypass traditional media and spread news of their brand through positive word-of-mouth.

Picture yourself driving along back country roads heavily populated by herds of brown and black cows. As you pass farm after farm, those individual cows quickly blend into one massive herd of boring, mind-numbing bovinity. They all look the same. Suddenly, you pass one farm that has a single purple cow standing in its field. That cow instantly captures your attention. Stands out from the rest of the herd. Stops you in your tracks.

Godin argued that the same dynamic applies whenever a customer travels down the metaphorical country road of any category where average or mediocre marketers extol generic virtues of ordinary brown and black cows. It's why all providers look and sound the same. Each town offers a plethora of lookalike accounting firms, law firms, corner bakeries, auto repair shops, manufacturers, and management and engineering consultants. Each metropolis has its assortment of beauty salons, tattoo parlors, mortgage brokers, realtors, financial planners and wedding planners, all dotting the landscape like giant herds of monochromatic Holsteins. Many of these providers are very good at what they do. Very good indeed. But, sadly, they are not remarkable enough to warrant favorable reputations outside their local area code.

"Very good" is an expectation. Hardly worth mentioning. In the world of branding, "very good" is *udderly vanilla*. Physical Icons and Energy Boosters are two approaches any leader can use with intention to craft a *zag* and bring the metaphorical concept of a "purple cow" to life.

Tactics alone, however, are not enough.

More than anything, creating a *zag* demands a certain mindset.

Will you allow the possibility of some purple haze to infiltrate and percolate through your brain? Do you have a mindset determined to create a one-of-a-kind original, rather than a second-hand copy? In their own, completely distinctive styles, Pike Place Fish Market, Webers on Highway 11, Canada's Huggable Car Dealer, Dollar Shave Club and the Savannah Bananas all found ways to make remarkable physical impressions and energetic human connections—both online and off.

Producing your own purple cow is not a paint-by-number, boilerplate process. Nor is it something you can just pick up at your local marketing firm's drive-thru window or discover through empirical, data-driven market research. Don't ever expect a customer focus group to tell you how to surprise them. What John Yokoyama discovered in 1986 is just as relevant today. Cutting through the noise is impossible when you use the same tactics as your competition. Taking a conservative approach means you won't get noticed—you'll get ignored. Boring is highly risky. It's much safer to *zag*.

While there are no guarantees that an outlandishly purple brainwave will work, it helps to know science is on your side when creating Physical Icons and Energy Boosters.

The Currency (and Science) of Attention

The scarcest resource for any business leader in our information-flooded world is not new ideas, raw materials, minerals, technology or talent. It's a pair of first cousins called Attention and Connection. If you are able to capture attention and hold it long enough to make a genuine human connection, you will increase your chances of inspiring the necessary level of trust that is required for any commercial exchange.

In scientific terms, "attention" is defined as the cognitive process of selectively concentrating on one thing while ignoring other things. "Connection," meanwhile, is the energy exchange that happens when people give attention to one another, unleashing invisible forces that deepen the moment and form emotional bonds. In many respects, Pike Place Fish Market, Webers on Highway 11, *Pawn Stars* and the Louvre are metaphorical laboratories for studying real-time consumer behavior. It's where you can make first-hand observations on how attitudes, feelings, biochemical reactions, buying decisions and the Mona Lisa Effect are influenced by factors such as the staying power of Strategic Drama, a prominent Physical Icon or the presence of an Energy Booster.

John and his fish-tossing team may not have plumbed the depths of the neuroscience of attention and connection, but their illustrious track record of business success illustrates what neuroscientist Antonio Damasio once observed: "We are not thinking machines that feel, we are feeling machines that think."

Feelings happen before thought, and they happen much faster. Our decision-making processes are far less rational and much more instinctual than we might care to admit. When you observe the throngs who divert their attention to the Pike Place Fish Market or join in the fun of the Savannah Bananas, it's easy to detect the wave of oxytocin-laden emotions, feelings and opinions that affect decision-making and generate lasting memories—positive or negative. We may prefer to think of ourselves as logical, level-headed human beings, but the vast majority of buying decisions are still prompted by subconscious impulses from our "reptilian brain." Multiple studies confirm that all aspects of storytelling, including live performance, music, celebration and theater, have the potential to kick our craniums into high gear. Especially when you hit the tripwire of a pair of tiny, almond-shaped sets of neurons located deep in the brain's medial temporal lobe—known as the amygdala.

Think of the amygdala as a set of front-row tickets to a Broadway production starring Attention and Connection. Like a curtain going up, the amygdala sends you an alert signal when it's activated. In his book *Brain Rules*, molecular biologist John Medina explains that when the brain detects an emotionally charged event or object, the amygdala releases dopamine into our systems. That dopamine greatly aids memory and information processing— explaining why a significant number of amygdala-charged Pike Place visitors or Savannah Banana fans repeat the story to their friends or jump on social media to share their experiences with strangers.

As the gatekeeper of our emotions, the amygdala is only one synapse away from the hippocampus, our memory center. This is why you clearly remember your first kiss, or the day you held your child for the first time. It's why you can't forget where you were on 9/11 or on the day man first walked on the moon. When an event triggers strongly felt emotions, we recall those memories much more clearly and vividly, and for longer periods of time.

Reflecting on that 2016 visit to Seattle, it's easy to recall a dozen or so competing vendors selling the same Pacific salmon, arctic char and wild Alaskan halibut. But only at the World Famous Pike Place Fish Market can you observe endless crowds of raving fans eager to snap selfies and evangelize on their behalf.

Humans with fully operational, fully functioning amygdalae are seldomly stirred at deep emotional levels by discount coupons, telemarketers, extended warranties or email blasts. They will, however, rally around brands that aren't afraid to go a little crazy, be a little silly, stand apart, play on the edge and make a real human connection. Logic and data may inform people, but it doesn't always incite action in the form of positive buying behaviors. We're much more inclined to act when the story is staged with larger-than-life bravado like Hendrix at Monterey, or speaks to patriotic hearts like President John F. Kennedy delivering his famous moon speech on September 12, 1962, at Rice University in Houston.

JFK's address was designed to persuade the American people to support NASA's Apollo program and place a man on the moon. At the time, the U.S. was losing the space race to the Soviets. There were loud public grumblings over the cost-benefit value of this mission.

"But, why, some say, the moon?" Kennedy asked. "Why choose this as our goal? And they may well ask, why climb the highest mountain? Why, 35 years ago, fly the Atlantic? Why does Rice play Texas? We choose to go to the moon in this decade and do the other things, not because they are easy, but because they are hard; because that goal will serve to organize and measure the best of our energies and skills, because that challenge is one that we are willing to accept, one we are unwilling to postpone, and one we intend to win."

Kennedy's vision was posthumously realized on July 20, 1969, with the success of Apollo 11. His frank, no-nonsense yet aspirational words became an Energy Booster that rallied the American people and the scientific community, evoking a pioneering spirit to explore the frontiers of space.

JFK, Jimi Hendrix, John Yokoyama and Jesse Cole each proved in their own unique way that audiences big and small will gladly give you their attention if you do something to earn it—and keep following through. Once you have triggered the dopamine-charged amygdala of a single individual, that person's biological need to share what they have discovered functions as the next person's point of discovery. From Seattle to Savannah, if you can catch attention and create a positive connection, there's a better than even chance they will remember and recommend you forever.

Timeless Takeaways

#1. Energy is contagious. Spread it!

Positive energy breeds more energy in the other human beings walking around with phone cameras, all of whom can post, tweet and spread your brand story on your behalf. Jonah Berger, professor of marketing at Wharton and author of *Contagious*: *Why Things Catch On*, studied nearly 7,000 articles in the *New York Times* to determine what was special about those on the most-emailed list. Berger found that the more positive the article, the more likely it was to become viral.

Shifting human energy does not necessarily mean you need to be animated, boisterous or zany, or otherwise act like a juggling circus act. What if you made the least noise possible? Took a minimalistic approach? Stripped everything back to its barest form? While Hendrix cranked dangerous to 11 at Monterey, another Seattle-based act did the exact opposite when grunge rockers Nirvana went "Unplugged in NY" on MTV in 1993. Likewise, Houston-based researcher Brené Brown would never be considered outlandish or clownish, but her quietly poignant way of communicating is devastatingly effective. Brown's 2012 speech on the power of vulnerability generated over 40 million views, making it one of the top five most viewed TED Talks. Her 2019 Netflix performance also demonstrates how human energy can be transferred without being outrageous or over-the-top.

#2. Only purple cows and flying fish are shareworthy.

Sharing is caring. If no one is sharing, it means that not enough people care. Before any customer whips out their phone and takes a selfie to promote your brand, they need to see or feel something completely different. Without a meaningful and clearly understood *zag*, any talk of brand strategy is pointless. At some point, you'll need to examine whatever is considered "normal" in your competitive space—then do the exact opposite. It's impossible to stand out if you blend in.

The fish products offered at Pike Place Fish Market are the same as those being offered at a dozen or so nearby vendors. Forget trying to be just a little bit better that the rest; strive to become the "only." Throwing fish, wearing yellow tuxedos or flaming up a Fender guitar are vivid examples of Energy Boosters that create an unmistakable, purple-hued *zag* others will share.

#3. Remarkability never goes out of style.

Being remarkable will never be a passing fad or trend. When a product or service builds a reputation for being undeniably different, people can't help but talk about it. And they won't stop talking. For decades. As long as there are enough amygdala-equipped humans around to notice, there's a good chance the enterprise in question can be viable for quite some time.

In time, Jesse Cole's yellow tux, top hat and over-the-top rope antics may well prove to have the same legendary power as baseball's beloved Harry Caray. After learning his craft at small operations in Joliet, Illinois, and Kalamazoo, Michigan, Harry landed in St. Louis before settling in Chicago, where, for the better part of 53 seasons, his infectious enthusiasm made summers magical and memorable for millions in Middle America. With unabashed exuberance and unbridled optimism, he became a one-man soundtrack for America's Pastime and the incredible popularity of a sacred ritual at ballparks everywhere—all with one memorable call: *All right! Lemme hear ya! Ah-One! Ah-Two! Ah-Three!*

Bottom of the Ninth

"Take Me Out to the Ballgame" ranks #8 on the "Songs of the 20th Century" list. An obscure vaudeville tune, the song became part of American folklore when Harry Caray started belting out his lusty, off-key Energy Booster in 1982 after joining the Chicago Cubs. Besides electrifying the ballpark during the 7th Inning Stretch, Harry's legendary run on WGN and the mythology he created played a key role in boosting Cubs' fortunes on the balance sheet. The Cubs are now worth $3.1 billion, making them one of five big-league clubs to be valued at more than $3 billion. Former *Chicago Sun-Times* columnist Ron Rapoport observed that "Harry's impact on the Cubs franchise was immeasurable. He was the face of the franchise in a way no player could have been because players didn't stay that long; they came and went, especially in that era. But Harry was there forever."

Harry Caray passed away in 1998, but his legacy and spirit lives on beyond the ivy-covered walls of iconic Wrigley Field. Currently, seven Windy City restaurants bear his name and likeness.

When things catch on, we often assume that the success happened overnight and out of the blue. Truth be told, great ideas gain traction one performance, one believer at a time. You only earn the right to connect with more people by delighting the first one.

For too long, too many marketers have been obsessed with tangible measurement. Clicks, follows, votes, transactions, bums in seats. Things that can be seen, counted and compared. But how do we measure the metrics of remarkability? How can we quantify the intangibles—evidenced or experienced over time—that are the backbone of strong relationships, cheerful customers, vibrant communities or any Big Little Legend?

The brand you lead has two possible destinies: be remarkable, or be invisible. You're either attracting attention or being ignored. The only variable is time.

The passage of time represents the difference between the decades Pike Place Fish Market has been reaping healthy profits by standing apart from the rest of the category versus the price being paid month after month by a business that won't be seen until its owner learns to see. Few ever stop to calculate the cost of being the same as everybody else.

Legends never emerge from being marginally better than their competitors, or even from simply being "very good." That's not the right path if you want fans to show up early and fight for a place in line. From jubilant fishmongers in Seattle, Washington, to canary-colored Bananas in Savannah, Georgia, there are always creative methods to shift energy and inspire customer love, no matter how dull or stale your industry, product or service.

If you try to be everything to everybody, you'll likely wind up being nobody to anyone and everyone.

Are you prepared to make a deliberate yet daring decision to reject conformity and being ordinary? Will you act with intention and do whatever it takes to make customers crush, swoon and fall head over heels in love with your brand?

Because as sure as God made green apples, the energy of *love* always beats the hell out of *like*.

Excuse me while I kiss the sky.

JIMI HENDRIX

6

BRANDING VOODOO IN THE BIG EASY

The Sweet Science of Sugary Generosity

September 10, 1866

Certain dialects in the English language are so uncommon they become mythological in a way that rivals the Loch Ness Monster. You can't see it, but you know it's there. One such dialect, unique to the city of New Orleans, is locally referred to as "Yat."

Derived from the phrase "where y'at?," this unmistakable language strongly resembles the speech pattern of someone from working-class Brooklyn, with plenty of *dose* and *dems*. It's not the southern country twang you might expect from a state that borders on Mississippi. From the region's first influx of migrants centuries ago, French Creoles and English rum runners mixed with enslaved Africans and immigrants from the West Indies. Toss in Germans, Italians, the Irish and others, and before you know it, NOLA dialects become one big melting pot of tasty Cajun jambalaya. Few cities on the planet vividly encapsulate the mix of the Old World with the New with one signature expression like the Big Easy.

Do whatcha wanna.

It's a local saying that captures the live-and-let-live spirit of New Orleans. A non-judgmental way of saying, let your freak flag fly, so long as you don't cause harm to others. Because here on the banks of the mighty Mississippi, nobody really cares if you use the full range of rainbow markers to color outside the lines.

Another word distinct to the New Orleans area is *lagniappe*.

Lagniappe (pronounced LAN-yap) is a creole word meaning "the gift" or "to give more." The custom dates back to French merchants of the 1840s, and is still widely practiced. Street vendors routinely throw in a few green chili peppers or a small bunch of cilantro with your purchase. Think of it as a "little extra" in a city where there is no such thing as excess. The epicenter of this overly generous, free-spirited street culture is found in the historic French Quarter. One bastion of that charitable urbanity can be discovered at a frequently visited landmark near historic Jackson Square on Decatur Street. This otherwise ordinary coffee shop with an extraordinary past attracts an unusually high volume of customers—without resorting to any traditional form of advertising.

For decades, the Mona Lisa Effect has been on full display at the Big Little Legend known as Café du Monde. Long lines of customers form here, all anxious to grab a seat at one of the 98 tables in this open-air café. An endless parade of newsmakers and celebrities have gone out of their way to pay a visit—U.S. presidents, movie stars like Ashton Kutcher and Reese Witherspoon, entertainers like Jay Leno, pro athletes like Joe Montana and Serena Williams, WWE stars and an assortment of Kardashians. You never know who you're going to see when you visit Café du Monde, otherwise known as "the original French Quarter coffee stand."

Serving only one food item and open 24/7, 364 days a year (they close for Christmas), Café du Monde defies all logic when it comes to accepted standards of the restaurant business. You won't see many diners staring at their phones while ignoring tablemates. What you will see is people engrossed in conversation, enjoying the open-air experience— and when they do pull out their phones, it's to upload visual content from their visit: a perpetual, word-of-mouth hurricane from the mouth of the Mississippi.

Tourists don't just eat beignets at Café du Monde. They tell stories about the experience when they get home ... but why? On social media, it's common to see posts that speak of near-orgasmic tastebud joy reminiscent of that famous scene from *When Harry Met Sally*. . . So, how did this cyclone of endless referrals get started? How did Café du Monde become such a "must-see" attraction in the Crescent City?

The Stickiest Brand in the Big Easy

Spend any time in New Orleans and you'll discover it's damn difficult to get a straight answer about precisely when the lines began to form at Café du Monde. The current owners of the business can't give you a definitive answer or logical explanation. Not even the almighty, all-knowing Google can solve this mystery. Research can provide reams of historical facts and figures but can't pinpoint a conclusive reason as to why this particular coffee shop became a bucket list destination for hundreds of thousands each year. It's a word-of-mouth riddle wrapped in an enigma. Unless you think there's merit to the tale of a 65th birthday celebration for a former leading citizen renowned for supernatural powers of witchcraft, magick and mastery of the occult.

Born in the French Quarter in the fall of 1801, the illegitimate daughter of a wealthy Creole plantation owner may have been at least partially responsible for some of the otherworldly success enjoyed by Café du Monde. Before digging into her story, consider these undisputable facts:

- Prior to the Civil War, the port of New Orleans was a major hub for the coffee industry, with imports streaming in from Latin America. In 1862, Fred Koeniger hopped on that wave, opening a new coffee stand so patrons could indulge in java with fried donuts while shopping at the market.

- In May 1942, Hubert Fernandez purchased the coffee stand and the business has remained in his family ever since.

- The only food item served at Café du Monde is a deep-fried sugared pastry treat called a beignet. When the Acadian people from Nova Scotia were expelled from Canada in the 18th century and migrated south, they brought with them French customs, such as Mardi Gras and the beignet.

- Beignets are not donuts, but squared pieces of dough with no hole in the middle, covered with powdered icing sugar about ten times finer than what you typically find at grocery stores. These light, puffy, golden brown pillows from food heaven send palates into a decadent dance with a long-lasting afterglow.

- In true lagniappe fashion, Café du Monde lays that fine icing sugar on extra-thick, so much so that a snowy dusting coats every visible part of your clothing. The powdered sugar is piled so high that you could visualize swooping down on it on a pair of skis. The frosted excess is an essential part of the customer experience, along with the chicory-flavored coffee that adds a chocolatey taste to the café au lait.

These beignets hold a clue to our puzzle, or at least part of the answer we're searching for. What if the secret lies in those extra scoops, the abundantly generous helpings of powdered sugar? And is it possible this expression of lagniappe also inspired supernatural forces to smile favorably upon Café du Monde shortly after it opened its doors at the height of the Civil War? Could the lavish spirit of generosity still be flowing from the ghostly soul of a widowed, free woman of color? A devout Catholic and one of America's most influential practitioners of voodoo, witchcraft and magick?

The subject of many songs, films and legends, Madame Marie Laveau is an enrapturing character and one of the bayou's unofficial cultural figureheads. Her story is often told—and never gets old.

The Voodoo Queen from New Orleans

Built by the Spanish in 1771, the building housing the original Café du Monde still stands directly across the street from Saint Louis Cemetery and the gravesite of the legendary priestess who made the shop famous. Although scores of other cafés populate the French Quarter and historic surrounding neighborhoods, none is more recognized than Café du Monde.

An African American healer of astounding beauty, Madame Marie Laveau was said to have wielded tremendous power within some of New Orleans' most influential circles. Fables of her magick abilities endure to this day, drawing visitors to pay homage at her tomb and leave amulets and tokens in exchange for asked favors.

The daughter of wealthy businessman and a woman who was born enslaved, Marie Laveau was the first generation of her family to be born free. While still in her late teens, she began combining her mother's African voodoo with Catholic traditions such as holy water, incense, candles and prayers, leading gatherings that attracted a wide range of people. Marie Laveau also saw wealthy clients on an individual basis, dispensing advice on everything from lawsuits to lovers. Feared for her dark powers, she read fortunes, performed exorcisms and other rituals to help rich and poor gain fame and fortune, become pregnant or exact revenge. Upon her death in 1881, her obituary in the *New York Times* claimed that "lawyers, legislators, planters and merchants all came to pay their respects and seek her offices."

According to local legend, Marie Laveau was also a devoted and loyal customer of Café du Monde. On our visit there in January 2019, a local man—cautious in the telling, lest he disturb the spirit of Marie Laveau—told us a story that had been passed down for generations within his hardscrabble Louisiana family—and could define the exact moment that the café started on the road toward becoming a legend.

> The tale we've heard since we were young'ins was that Marie Laveau loved those beignets and all that icing sugar so much that she cast a spell of white magic on the coffee shop.
>
> As the story goes, she cast the spell on her 65th birthday, on September 10, 1866. Marie Laveau knew she was getting on in years and wanted the owners of Café du Monde to attract an eternal bounty of happy paying customers who loved their tasty beignets as much as she did. Before she died in 1881, she made a point of telling the owners at the time about the incantations she done on their behalf and that she be protectin' the café from her place in heaven, hell or wherever God was sending her in the afterlife.

There is plenty of information about Marie Laveau and stories of her hexes and charms, but separating hard facts from Delta mythology has always been a challenge. Everything known about her originates from secretive oral traditions of voodoo practitioners, liberally sprinkled and embellished with hearsay and drama. Layer in real-life stories like the

1982 arrest of punk rockers The Misfits after they went graveyard hunting for her final resting place, and her already larger-than-life persona becomes even more intriguing.

While impossible to verify or dispute the story of the birthday benediction in '66, there is no denying that Marie Laveau was a Louisiana legend in her own time, a saintly figure who nursed the sick and prayed for the condemned. Some believe she still wields paranormal powers from the grave that lies across the street. There is, however, another and more likely reason the popularity of Café du Monde as it mushroomed across New Orleans and beyond. In all probability it had something to do with the enticing aroma of those tasty beignets and how it lured hard-working long-shoremen like bees to flowers back in early years of the café's existence.

Growing up in the French Quarter, Chic Miller of Toast-masters International learned as a boy that the café's word-of-mouth popularity may have been helped by its prime location next to a busy commercial waterfront. Miller recounts how stevedores working 12- to 14-hour shifts would pop by for what would have been the equivalent of downing multiple Red Bulls during the Civil War era. The mix of sweet, sugar-fried pastry with high-octane caffeine was the perfect mid-day jolt hearty workhands needed before heading back to the docks and handling heavy cargo. Ample traces of frosted evidence still covered their work clothes. People noticed. Folks talked. And voila! Word began to spread through the Quarter and beyond. Café du Monde was in the right place at the perfect time.

Abundant Generosity and the Spirit of Reciprocity

Besides Physical Icons and Energy Boosters, the word-of-mouth trifecta any leader can budget and plan for is completed by delightfully sincere gestures of Abundant Generosity.

The timeless principle of reciprocity has led to a hard-wired social expectation that people will respond to each other in kind. When people or companies do us a good turn, something in our DNA tugs at us to return the favor. It's an unwritten social construct that holds cultures together.

In the 1980s, psychology expert Dr. Robert Cialdini, author of *Influence*, helped marketing strategists widely adopt the free-sampling tactic that soon became a craze. Think of your last trip to Costco—did you end up with an unplanned Mexican taco or Bavarian sausage purchase because you felt obligated to buy after a friendly server tempted you try a couple of those juicy bites for free? As Dr. Cialdini explains, "People are obliged to give back to others the form of a behavior, gift or service that they have received first. If a friend invites you to their house party, there's an unwritten obligation for you to return the favor at a future party you are hosting." If somebody at work covers for you or helps you meet a deadline, you're more inclined help them out when they're in a jam. In the context of social obligation, people are more likely to say yes to those who they feel indebted to.

There is no question that this approach drives sales. Legendary brands, however, are not built simply by dangling a few free carrots or an extra thick slice of key lime pie. Reciprocity in the form of free subscriptions, free consultations, free test drives or a free warm cookie at a hotel check-in desk is an expectation. As the world became more skeptical, some of these approaches began to cast a certain odor.

They started smelling like a greasy bait-and-switch tactic reeking of desperation and manipulation. Building a one-of-a-kind irresistible brand—one that ignites the Mona Lisa Effect—forces leaders to think beyond bare minimums like free bottled water, a monthly newsletter or writing a check to tick the box called corporate social responsibility.

The secret to inspiring self-appointed brand evangelists is to make generosity visibly and rampantly abundant. No strings attached.

At Café du Monde, they pour on lagniappe like there is no tomorrow. The copious amount of sugar on those beignets is at least three to four times larger than it needs to be. Their pastries are so lavishly smothered with white powder that any bean-counting bookkeeper could make a convincing argument that Café du Monde could cut its annual sugar budget in half without compromising on quality. However, that type of spreadsheet thinking would asphyxiate the brand. For the sake of saving a few nickels, it would eliminate and eradicate the essential ingredient creating customer magic.

Those bountiful extra scoops of icing sugar are a key component of the word-of-mouth strategy at Café du Monde. Dishing out lagniappe on steroids increases the odds that customers will be walking billboards while meandering through the French Quarter.

Oh... I see you went to Café du Monde. How were dose beignets dis morning? Were dey that good that ya had to wear 'em? Ha ha!

Chic Miller believes the same dynamic occurred with 19th-century longshoremen. When they went back to the docks, they also bumped into crewmen from ships all over the world. Frosted clothing became a delightful topic of conversation. Impossible not to notice. Before long, international visitors were flocking to Café du Monde, enjoying those delectable French Acadian treats and spreading word-of-mouth marketing magic. Was that how Madame Marie Laveau herself found out about dose beignets?

But, what if there is a science-based perspective that also explains why Abundant Generosity has such an impact on human behaviors?

Lay It on Thick. Let Science Spread the Word.

Of the more than 30 scientific and medical studies reviewed during the research for this book, several stand out.

Researchers at the University of Pittsburgh, for example, discovered in 2018 that a generous act has the power to turn the dial down on the brain's natural anxiety center. In other words, the automatic fight-or-flight response all but disappears in the face of Abundant Generosity, allowing happy chemicals like endorphins, dopamine and serotonin to flood our systems. Meanwhile, the neuroeconomics department at the University of Zurich used MRI testing to pinpoint specific areas of our brains that are impacted during times of generosity. Simply put, the temporoparietal junction (TPJ) is the community-minded part of our brain associated with social cognition, empathy and thinking of others. When you are on the receiving end of a generous act, your TPJ lights up like a Christmas tree. Simultaneously, the self-centered, greedy part of your brain, otherwise known as the ventral striatum, is kicked into sleep mode.

The Zurich studies also explain what is known as the "Warm Glow Effect"—the warm and fuzzy feelings we experience when we do something good for someone else. Entering Café du Monde is like walking into a real-life human laboratory that explains the compounding power of lagniappe in scientific terms. You can only imagine what would happen to a workplace team at the neurochemical level if everyone punching the clock experienced the Warm Glow Effect consistently.

Eventually, someone did imagine that possibility. And turned that idea into a billion-dollar buyout.

Few companies have embraced the spirit of Abundant Generosity like Zappos. The Las Vegas–based online shoe retailer has never spent big bucks on advertising, preferring to delight one customer at a time. Visionary founder Tony Hsieh felt that, rather than investing in ads, it made more sense to create generously abundant personal experiences and let Zappos customers do word-of-mouth marketing about all their unexpected perks.

Unlike the vast majority of call center operations, Zappos agents never use scripts. They never upsell. The company doesn't fret over processing high call volumes or executing quick-time resolutions. As culture evangelist Jon Wolske explained, "It's more important that we make an emotional connection with the customer, rather than just quickly getting them off the phone." Together with Tony and other Zappos leaders, Jon helped design company tours that would attract more than a thousand people a month—tours where visitors could experience that feeling in real life. They offered classes to teach other business executives how to create highly engaged workplaces, including their year-long process of listening to every employee before distilling their culture into ten core values.

There are too many stories to tell about that Zappos generosity, but one worth mentioning occurred in November 2015 in a small New Hampshire town. While not a creature was stirring, a team of 30 enthusiastic Zapponian elves descended upon Hanover, New Hampshire, to deliver happiness in the form of holiday gift boxes to nearly 2,000 doorsteps. Inside those packages were cold-weather gear like hats, gloves, wool socks, backpacks and more to equip folks for the northeastern winter. Hanover was a small community with a high percentage of customers particularly loyal to Zappos, and years later people still talk about that day when a little lagniappe went a long way.

Before perishing at age 46 in a tragic 2020 house fire, Tony Hsieh wrote a bestselling book, *Delivering Happiness*, that further revealed the Zappos secret culture sauce in order to help other companies—including competitors—do better business. Jon Wolske could fill your ear with stories about Zappos employees helping customers find the closest pizza place, day care facility and more. In 2009, Amazon purchased Zappos for $1.2 billion, which raised eyebrows, since Amazon sold the same products online for lower prices. But what Amazon was really buying was a *brand*, one that had established the industry's gold standard for customer care and generosity. Tony Hsieh has insisted from the beginning that Zappos is "a customer service company that just happens to sell shoes." Hardly surprising that 75% of Zappos orders come from returning customers.

Plenty of other high impact brands have reaped the rewards of Abundant Generosity. Originating in Vancouver in 1998, Lululemon organizes free yoga and fitness classes on a weekly basis, enlisting the support of yoga teachers and fitness trainers that choose to embody the brand's values and lifestyle. Those instructors become brand ambassadors, outfitted with free gear while promoting their own yoga and fitness programs. There isn't a content marketer alive who doesn't offer free videos, tip sheets or ebooks, but few have been as prolific, consistent and wildly generous as *New York Times*-bestselling author Roy H. Williams with his weekly "Monday Morning Memo." Founder of the world-famous Wizard Academy, Williams began his flagship memo when he freely shared his unique insights to a global audience through a fax machine as far back at the late 1980s.

To this day, Dana and I have never forgotten the story we heard from our friends Mike and Roberta Garrity about their trip to a Chicago conference, where they saw Blake Mycoskie telling a story that started with his second-place finish in *The Amazing Race* in Argentina. Hanging on their every word, we listened as our lunchmates went into great detail, re-telling how Blake discovered that many

Argentinian children could not attend school because they had no shoes. Blake went back to Santa Monica and in 2006 launched his own shoe company from his apartment—one with a novel idea. For every pair of shoes sold, he would donate a pair to a child in need. An early example of social entrepreneurship, Blake's brainchild, TOMS Shoes, has since donated more than 95 million shoes in more than 85 countries while generating a profit and sustaining its mission.

It wasn't through traditional marketing and advertising that we first learned about the magic of TOMS. It was through the sincere sharing of a story from trusted friends in the spirit of Abundant Generosity. If imitation is the sincerest form of flattery: the TOMS "One for One" giving model has been adopted by many others, such as vision care company Warby Parker, which donates a pair of their eyeglasses for every one sold. After the 2018 shootings in Thousand Oaks, California, TOMS expanded its purpose-driven mission by donating $5 million for programs to end gun violence and inspiring 750,000 Americans to send postcards to their congressperson urging them to pass universal background checks.

At Jim Gilbert's Wheels & Deals, the principle of Abundant Generosity happens every time one of the more than 15,000 members of the Huggable Birthday Club goes to their mailbox and finds a gift. Launching the program in 1998 with handwritten and handmade cards from a desktop printer, the Gilberts have compiled a list of all current and former customers, who continue to receive a birthday present each year—even if they haven't bought a car for decades.

That generous community spirit was even more apparent at the height of the 2020 global pandemic. Jim and Dawna's daughter Chelsea Gilbert and daughter-in-law Chelsey Wyman-Gilbert launched an initiative to distribute snacks and lunches to Fredericton-area schools and kindergartens faced with supply shortages. With mascots in tow, the leaders from Canada's Huggable Car Dealer stepped up to serve and make people smile in a time of need.

Meanwhile, Café du Monde keeps laying it on thick with extra scoops of lagniappe: heaps of sugary white magic that sustain their bewitching allure. In a world of rapid change, we find comfort and peace with brands that give us the sense of permanence and stability often missing from our chaotic lives. Physical Icons, Energy Boosters and Abundant Generosity help establish true and meaningful differentiation while connecting with deep-rooted human needs and values.

For generations, icons such as Apple, Ferrari, Nike and Disney—along with all the Big Little Legends profiled so far—have consistently demonstrated a timeless truism about brand building. It's a well-established fact, supported by science, that humans buy not from their brains but from their *hearts*. Only in our hearts do our stories of myths and legends handed down for generations reside.

Prior to personally experiencing the flavorsome delights of Café du Monde, it would have been impossible for us to see the connection between heavily powdered beignets and one of the most iconic rock bands in music history. In his 2020 bestseller *Fanocracy*, author and speaker David Meerman Scott recounts how attending more than 800

live music concerts—including 75 that featured The Grateful Dead—led to an inescapable conclusion: *When we give to
others rather than take, we develop a fanocracy.*

In his book, David and his daughter (and fellow fandom
expert) Reiko Scott define a fanocracy as an "organization that inspires extreme passion for a product, service or
idea by putting customer's needs and wishes at the center
of everything it does; a force critical for massive success."
From their early San Francisco beginnings, The Grateful
Dead refused to hide behind gatekeepers. Readily accessi-
ble, the Dead encouraged an open dialogue and even placed
a direct call-to-action inside 1971's *Skull and Roses*, asking
fans to reach out and connect:

> DEAD FREAKS UNITE: Who are you? Where are you?
> How are you? Send us your name and address and we'll
> keep you informed. Deadheads, P.O. Box 1065, San
> Rafael, California 94901

Within six months, the band received 10,257 responses.
Within five years, 63,147 Deadheads had requested to
receive regular mailings from the band. Long before Facebook and YouTube, the band was building their own social
networks through Abundant Generosity.

An outlier in the music industry, the Dead poured their
efforts into nonstop touring and permitted fans (Deadheads)
to tape their shows and circulate their music freely without
demanding royalties. Most record companies and musicians were adamantly opposed to this approach, thinking it
would infringe on copyright and destroy industry revenue

models, but the exact opposite occurred. Instead of shutting down or filing lawsuits against makers of bootleg tie-dye T-shirts or homemade cassette tapes, the Dead formed partner projects that permitted vendors to produce their own band paraphernalia and share in the profits. At concert venues, the band welcomed charitable organizations to set up tables and educate music fans on issues like organ donation, nature conservation and voter registration.

Essentially, the Dead's insistence on substance over style has ensured steady profit streams that still roll in. In 2020, Nike released a limited-edition shoe with a psychedelic design inspired by the back cover of *History of the Grateful Dead, Volume One*. The line sold out immediately. The shoes now fetch about $1,500 on eBay.

What started with concert tees emblazoned with the Stealie (the band's iconic skull and lightning bolt logo) to key chains, condiments and Cherry Garcia ice cream, an entire nation of Dead-centric boomer stockbrokers, doctors, dentists and lawyers proudly wear Jerry Garcia ties to the office. By allowing fans to freely record and share their live music, the Dead fostered a unique, diehard fan culture—a fanatical following that weathered the internet-fueled music industry crisis and fickleness of the entertainment world for decades. Thousands of other rock "brands" came and went while the Dead translated Abundant Generosity into a cash cow for generations.

Timeless Takeaways

#1. A giving spirit creates rock-steady currency.

Besides hard scientific evidence that sincere altruism boosts personal energy while decreasing stress and anxiety, there is a business case to be made for how good deeds benefit the bottom line. But it only kicks in when we acknowledge the universe as truly abundant: tapping into a spiritual dimension multiplies our being and our results.

According to Fred Reichheld, author of *The Ultimate Question: Driving Good Profits and True Growth*, a 12% increase in brand advocacy on average generates a 2x increase in revenue growth while boosting overall market share. In other words, every time a customer tells a friend about their Café du Monde experience or posts another selfie with a beignet, the impact is felt at the cash register. What creative ways could you use to share Abundant Generosity with your customers, team, community or causes that hit close to home?

#2. The more you give, the more it grows.

The term "abundance" comes from the Latin *abundantia*, which means "overflowing riches." It contains within it the idea of limitless possibility.

When you give, others notice and become inspired to give more. Those who receive become more generous, which begets a chain reaction of giving with no expiry date. At their height, The Grateful Dead pulled in as much as $95 million a year, not just from concert tickets and record sales, but also from an ever-multiplying roster of spinoff products. As they eschewed mainstream music industry promotion and splashy ad campaigns, giving back to the community became integral to their image. Founding member Jerry Garcia passed away a month after the original band played its final show at Chicago's Soldier Field on July 9, 1995, but his legacy lives on. Whether it was music or merch, the Dead allowed content to spread. Without barriers.

#3. Doing good makes you feel damn great!

Charles Dickens once wrote, "No one is useless in this world who lightens the burden of another." Regardless of what neuroscientists from Pittsburgh to Zurich have discovered, you can test the Warm Glow Effect for yourself at any drive-thru window. Next time you fork over a $10 bill to pay for coffee for the strangers behind you, pay close attention to how it affects your own emotional state. Start to imagine how any business and brand could replicate that experience of creating joy in someone's day from a pure, no-strings-attached point of view. How would you prepare the ingredients and start cooking up your own kind of inspirational soup for your company's soul?

Abundant Generosity is not about following a list of boilerplate instructions or "7 Easy Steps."

This is not a gimmick to trick algorithms or adopting a cookie-cutter formula. It's about following what your heart knows to be true and taking a leap of faith in much the same manner as Café du Monde, Canada's Huggable Car Dealer, Zappos, Lululemon or The Grateful Dead. It's incredibly powerful to give something with no expectation of anything in return, like leaving $50 on the pillow for the hard-working people who clean your hotel room. It must be genuine, otherwise the gesture will feel like coercion, similar to the many B2B companies who offer a free white paper but require you to hand over your email address. To fully embrace Abundant Generosity, make it completely free and give yourself the chance to grow a steadfastly loyal fan base.

Good to the Last Drop

The voice of the customer has never been more potent or powerful.

How will your business and brand amplify that voice and create your own legions of diehard followers? With consumers increasingly connected to social media and equally suspicious about shady sales tactics and contrived marketing ploys, it helps to know most people still want to feel good about brands they support.

Forget drumming up hype or superficial buzz. Start thinking beyond the metaphorical beignet. With one food item and delicious roasted coffee, Café du Monde created a brand that became a shared community experience. A cultural icon smack in the middle of uncontested market space.

Defy convention. Make up your own rules. Give plenty more than you have to and let the *bon temps rouler!*

Embrace the voodoo of lagniappe, scientifically validated to be highly effective every day of the week and twice over on Sundays.

Especially in the Crescent City, where "Who Dat" Nation gathers at a cathedral called the Superdome to worship and pray for all dem Sinners and Saints.

America has only three cities:
New York, San Francisco and New Orleans.
Everywhere else is just Cleveland.

TENNESSEE WILLIAMS

PART III

MEDIUM + MESSAGE

7

BANG A TRIBAL DRUM

Will Your Battle Cry Rock the World?

November 2, 2018

The rhythm is equal parts tribal, primal and powerful.

Inclusive. Inspiring. Irresistible.

Stomp, stomp, clap! Stomp, stomp, clap! Stomp, stomp, clap!

The four-word chorus that follows is a call to arms for anyone who has ever been beaten down, shoved aside, discarded or ignored.

A wailing 45-second guitar solo takes it over the top rope.

Sitting in a darkened movie theater watching *Bohemian Rhapsody* on November 2, 2018, a single scene—a single moment, even—distilled down the entire essence of a principle I had been thinking about for weeks. During a recording session, Brian May, played by Gwilym Lee, exhorts his reluctant bandmates to encourage Queen fans to sing along at their live shows. May wants Queen's audience to feel like they are part of the band. He envisions sending more than 80,000 concertgoers into a unified frenzy with a simple, anthemic beat.

We will . . . we will . . . ROCK YOU!

Stripped down. Basic and bare.

Two minutes and one second of galvanizing boot stomping on a wooden drum riser, overlapped by thundering vocals from the legendary Freddie Mercury. This one scene from the Queen biopic perfectly illustrates how any business or brand benefits from having its own sonic equivalent to "We Will Rock You." Folks at one company headquartered in Beaverton, Oregon, would fist-pump and nod *hell yeah*. Their brand has been well served since 1988 with a three-word statement that packs a similar aural punch. That statement became a unifying proclamation for everyone from Olympic athletes to suburban walkers as the company boosted its share of the North American sport-shoe business from 18% to 43% over a ten-year period.

Just Do It.

Jim Gilbert acknowledges that he enjoyed a similar bottom-line impact with the four key words that became the foundation for all his marketing efforts. An evocative phrase that altered public perception and inspired higher levels of trust.

Canada's Huggable Car Dealer.

In the mid-1980s, the department of transportation in Texas (known as TxDOT) launched a public awareness campaign designed to reduce littering on state highways. Within two years, the amount of roadside trash decreased by 72%. The state also hit the jackpot, collecting royalties on a multi-million-dollar merchandising business that practically fell into their ten-gallon hats, thanks to four carefully chosen words.

Don't Mess With Texas.

When the late Steve Jobs returned from corporate exile and rejoined a nearly bankrupted company in 1997, he rallied Apple's leadership team around a new, two-word brand story and vision. At an internal meeting on September 23, 1997, Jobs revealed a grainy, black-and-white TV spot featuring icons such as Albert Einstein, Thomas Edison, Amelia Earhart, Pablo Picasso, the Muppets and Muhammad Ali: a visual and poetic salute to misfits, rebels and troublemakers who saw the world differently. The final two words in that 60-second masterpiece was the stirring call to action that transformed a corporate laughingstock into a stock anyone would dream of owning.

Think Different.

Each case—Nike, Jim Gilbert's Wheels & Deals, TxDOT, Apple—demonstrates how a strategically crafted two-to-six-word phrase can go a long way toward rousing curiosity and emotions while making deep impressions and inspiring people to action. Metaphorically, these two to six words are equivalent to a hard-charging pet rhino. A short declaration that makes a larger, single point in a robustly clear and compelling way. A clannish call to arms that leaves room for interpretation and gives people something to chew on, talk about, debate and ruminate. Something easy to grasp, understand, recognize, share and repeat to others.

Such is the thundering force of the Tribal Narrative.

The origin of the word "tribe" stems way back to ancient Rome. The word *tribus* was used to describe the division of the state. As Europeans moved over the globe, it was used to describe the various cultures they encountered. In the study of anthropology, the word tribe is used to describe everything from forager bands and hunter-gatherer societies to larger groups, likes the Twelve Tribes of Israel, or even states or members of a given religious denomination. Think of it like a unifying rhythm or a connecting thread. Fuse that rhythm with a literary device—those powerful, precisely chosen two to six words—and you have the Tribal Narrative.

A distinctive Tribal Narrative combines the pulse of a stirring drumbeat with the emotional energy of a compelling story. Think of the impact of some of the best Tribal Narratives ever crafted:

Dollar Shave Club: "Shave Time. Shave Money."
De Beers: "A Diamond Is Forever."
City of Las Vegas: "What Happens in Vegas, Stays in Vegas."
California Milk Processor Board: "Got Milk?"
Charlesglen Toyota: "Alberta's Celebration Destination."
Parkville Manor: "Home of the Underage Senior."
Pool Troopers: "America's Backyard Heroes."
Ritz-Carlton: "Ladies & Gentlemen Serving Ladies & Gentlemen."
Road Runner Sports: "Make Every Mile Count."
Red Bull: "Gives You Wiiings."
Toronto Raptors: "We the North."
USMC: "The Few. The Proud. The Marines."

Equally appealing and relevant to customers, employees, leadership teams, fans and shareholders, two-to-six-word phrases like these can be the rock-solid foundation of a cohesive story that allows your brand to establish consistency, longevity and equity in the mind of the market.

A Tribal Narrative is not any common slogan or a tagline.

The vast majority of those are boring and ineffective. Often, they are a tragic waste of valuable branding real estate. Flavorless porridge. Recycled, re-heated, regurgitated platitudes with zero taste or panache.

Jones & Smith Insurance: "Reliable Insurance and Advice."
Jones & Smith Insurance: "Insurance Protection You Can Trust."
Jones & Smith Insurance: "Locally Owned Insurance Experts."

Such a mundane combination of words won't get anyone's pulse racing. Slim chance any of these phrases will ever appear on a T-shirt or a tattoo. The choice to use a motto straddling the line between humdrum and ordinary increases the odds that Jones & Smith will end up as white noise in their crowded, competitive market. Traditional boilerplate slogans or taglines, devoid of dramatic elements, are a surefire way to make your brand blend in with the rest. What you want is to unleash a rhino into the category jungle you occupy, driving curiosity, commanding attention and, hopefully, inspiring the Mona Lisa Effect for decades to come.

Make the Drum Talk

Thanks to how our brains are hardwired, humankind has always responded to timeless musical forces that can be traced back to the ancient drumming practices of the Mali Empire in Africa. Unlike Western societies, where drumming tends to be associated with entertainment, there is a deeper symbolic and historical meaning with this style of African drums.

For centuries, drums have been integral to African storytelling, passing on important historical, religious and cultural information to future generations or sending out a call to join a battle. The most skilled of these drummers in modern-day Mali in West Africa are known as the ones who "can make the djembe talk," meaning the player has a flair for telling an emotional story.

The basic construct of any Tribal Narrative lies in the judicious use of lyrical wording that echoes a rhythmic beat and fuses it with a dramatic proclamation that reflects any storyline from *The Seven Basic Plots*. In that respect, the Carolina Panthers NFL team provides a perfect illustration of how one story can shape a genuine brand narrative grounded in timeless, emotional truth.

Keep Pounding.

Two simple words from an emotional locker room speech that still serves as a permanent reminder of human values that live for eternity. Two words that have nothing to do with marketing.

Two words that had everything to do with the fighting spirit of a dying man who refused to roll over and quit.

These words were delivered by assistant coach and former player Sam Mills, who had just been diagnosed with intestinal cancer. Before the teams took the field in a playoff game against the Dallas Cowboys on January 2, 2004, Coach Mills wanted to speak. Players gathered tightly and took a knee. The linebacker coach informed the men that doctors had just given him three months to live. In a powerful but soft-spoken voice, he told them this:

When I found out I had cancer, there are two things I could have done. Quit and died or keep pounding. I'm a fighter. I kept pounding. You're all fighters too. So keep pounding! Keep pounding on offense! Keep pounding on defense! Keep pounding on special teams! Keep pounding on every single play!

On that frigid January day in 2004, Sam Mills made tough, battle-scarred men break down and weep.

That afternoon, the Panthers went out and defeated the favored Cowboys 29-10, and later won two more playoff games to capture the NFC Championship. They went on to make their first Super Bowl appearance against the New England Patriots, only to lose on a last-second field goal.

But Sam's message hasn't ended. If anything, it is only growing stronger.

Sam kept pounding as long as he could, long outlasting the doctors' forecast before finally succumbing at his Charlotte home on April 18, 2005. The former coach and All-Pro linebacker was 45. Few players and coaches in the Panthers locker room at that remarkable game could have predicted how two heartfelt words would inspire an entire organization, city, state and fan base for years to come.

Two words became his legacy.

"Keep Pounding" adorns the walls of the Panthers locker room, weight room and stadium hallways. "Keep Pounding" is stitched into the collar of every Carolina Panthers jersey, a permanent reminder from a coach and teammate who fought to the end with every means at his disposal. It's also Panthers tradition to select an honorary "Keep Pounding" drummer to bang a giant drum four times before each home game, signifying their willingness to fight for all four quarters. Sam's #51 jersey was retired prior to the Panthers' 2005 season. A bronze statue honoring his memory stands just outside the north entrance to Bank of America Stadium.

"Keep Pounding" became the name of a charitable foundation to fund cancer research programs in conjunction with Charlotte's Atrium Health Foundation. Through efforts that include the Keep Pounding 5K road race and other initiatives, the fund has raised millions of dollars for cancer research programs and patient support programs at Levine Cancer Institute and the Levine Children's Hospital. The warrior spirit of the mantra encourages cancer patients, survivors and their loved ones—along with their medical teams—to overcome obstacles and maintain faith that someday a cure will be found.

"Keep Pounding" is a Tribal Narrative that speaks to timeless, universal values that transcend wins, losses or anything else that happens on a football field. Nothing given. Everything earned with hard work, sweat equity and a combative attitude. Lay everything on the line, every day. Keep knocking on the door until it opens. Or kick the damn thing down.

Similar to what Nike and Queen fans experience, the Panthers' "Keep Pounding" is the eternal chant of the underdog, a rallying cry anchored by dramatic elements of the Overcoming the Monster plot. It's a classic example of how a Tribal Narrative can give your brand a foundation of emotional truth, derived from real events and characters. In the case of Canada's Huggable Car Dealer, the plots of Comedy and Voyage & Return are reflected back to the audience in a way that is associated with a Disneyesque experience. When Apple introduced "Think Different," it embodied the idea of the Quest along with an element of Rebirth: to let one's imagination run wild and work overtime in a crazy mission to change the world. "Don't Mess With Texas" offers tongue-in-cheek swagger and no-nonsense posture that falls under twin umbrellas of Comedy and Overcoming the Monster.

With a little bit of rhythm and a lot of soul—along with the framework of *The Seven Basic Plots*—any brand can employ a straight-from-the-heart Tribal Narrative that can establish consistency, longevity and a unique identity in the mind of the customer. In a nutshell, a properly crafted Tribal Narrative answers the essential, unspoken question in the mind of any customer: *Who are you, beyond what you sell?*

Dig Deeper, Soar Higher

Are you prepared to unearth what's original, real and raw? To explore sensitive emotional truths, painful scars, proud moments and glorious accomplishments that have been part of your personal journey? The triumphs, tragedies and embarrassing failures? Think of those crucially significant days in your personal history that shaped you, defined who you are, and how those events formed the shared values, vision and beliefs of your organization. What meaningful events explain why you do what you do?

For a Tribal Narrative to gain traction, it must rest on a mountain of core values. Not the ones described in so many wretched corporate mission statements. You need to find the *real* stuff, like the way one small company in the Pacific Northwest did when it faced this challenge in the mid-1960s.

An Oregonian through and through, Bill taught biology and coached football at Portland's Franklin High School before life changed forever when Japanese warplanes attacked the Pacific Fleet at Pearl Harbor on December 7, 1941. Like a lot of Americans of fighting age, Bill joined the military and served with General Mark Clark's U.S. Fifth Army, battling German forces during the Italian campaign. Bill, recently promoted to the rank of major, was leading a battalion of about 400 troops near the Brenner Pass in the Italian Alps when he encountered a situation straight out of a Hollywood movie. Facing a regiment of about 4,000 Nazi soldiers, Bill grabbed an interpreter, hopped in a jeep and approached an SS checkpoint. Using bluster and bluff, he demanded that the sentries take him to visit their commanding officer.

Bill was taking more than a calculated risk. However, he had trained as an officer to use "initiative appropriate to the situation." Once Bill was escorted across enemy lines to face the Nazi general—and many armed, fanatical SS guards—at his headquarters in the 15th-century Castel Toblino, he issued a simple demand. Either the Germans lay down their arms and surrender by 10 a.m. the next day, or they should prepare to engage in battle.

Within hours, Bill and his men were taking German prisoners in an orderly fashion, avoiding needless bloodshed and hastening the end of the war. It would not be the first that time Bill Bowerman would employ initiative, courage and resourcefulness to his advantage.

Upon returning home, the former citizen soldier launched a track and field coaching career that saw him train 64 All-Americans, 33 Olympians, 22 NCAA champions and 16 milers who broke the four-minute barrier. Bill was named head coach of Team USA at the '72 Munich Olympics, and over 24 seasons at the University of Oregon, his Ducks captured four NCAA titles and finished top ten in the nation 16 times. Fascinated by the concept of running as a fitness routine for people of all ages, Bill wrote a three-page guide called "A Jogger's Manual," which triggered a bestselling book widely credited for sparking America's love affair with jogging.

Obsessed with developing anything that would give his athletes an edge, Bill needed a guinea pig to test new running shoe designs. He reached out to one of his Oregon students, and Phil was more than happy to oblige. A capable runner himself, Phil knew the value of high-performance shoe equipment: how one ounce of support could mean 10,000 pounds of difference in the home stretch of a marathon. In fact, as a business student, Phil had written a paper titled "Can Japanese Sports Shoes Do to German Sports Shoes What Japanese Cameras Did to German Cameras?" Unlike most students, however, Phil turned his college paper into a real business. He and Bill partnered in 1964 and started selling imported Japanese shoes under the label Blue Ribbon Sports. The bond between coach and student and their shared obsession for precision, innovation and ingenuity was cemented with a handshake deal and $1,200 in start-up capital. Before long, they were at track meets sell-ing their wares out of the trunk of a green Plymouth Valiant.

In their first year of business, tiny BRS sold about 1,300 pairs of shoes, grossing about $8,000. They hardly caught the eye of global behemoths like Germany's Adidas or Puma, both of which were billion-dollar operations at the time. Like so many established incumbents in so many industries, these companies never saw the emerging threat from a future Big Little Legend.

Little by little, the diminutive company grew. On May 30, 1971, Blue Ribbon Sports changed their name and started manufacturing their own shoes with Bill's unique "waffle sole" design offering better traction with less weight. That shoe put them on the global athletic footwear map. Orig-inal employee Jeff Johnson thought they should name the company in honor of the Greek goddess of victory. The com-pany also commissioned a new logo that year from Portland State art student Carolyn Davidson for a fee of $35. Phil said he didn't like it, but he would get used to it. In 1972, they signed their first athlete endorsement contract with con-troversial bad-boy tennis professional Ilie Năstase. Oregon track star Steve Prefontaine followed in '73 and the com-pany went public on December 2, 1980, with shares trading at 18 cents.

In 1984 they took another calculated risk and bet the endorsement farm on an unproven college basketball player from North Carolina, signing him to a five-year deal worth $7 million. Stardom and immortality followed with Michael Jordan and the Chicago Bulls.

Long before waffle trainers, the "swoosh" logo and Air Jordan, Nike's internal culture was driven by a can-do attitude that honored what co-founder Bill had been saying for decades: "Everyone has a body and is therefore a potential athlete." In 1988, they translated that vision and the values of initiative, resourcefulness and athleticism into a simple yet profound Tribal Narrative. An anthem for everyday athletes everywhere, it defends the sacred values of sports and fitness while slaying mental dragons of excuses and inertia. Nike figured out a way to "make the djembe talk" with three one-syllable words.

Just Do It.

Just Tell the Truth

According to the Center for Applied Research, the iconic Nike narrative was born in a 1988 meeting with the Wieden+Kennedy advertising agency. At the meeting, ad exec Dan Wieden was infected by the rah-rah, gung-ho spirit of the company and reportedly complimented Phil Knight's executive team, saying, "You Nike guys, you just do it." Later, Dan acknowledged that some of his inspiration may have been derived from the last words of convicted killer and Portland native Gary Gilmore, who uttered "Let's do it" before being executed in Utah. There is also a chance he was influenced by a public service campaign from Nancy Reagan when America's First Lady encouraged youth to "Just Say No" to drugs.

Whatever Dan's inspiration, mash these phrases together and you have storytelling continuity for Nike commercials that has ranged from running to walking, cross-training to basketball, golf to skateboarding and everything in between. The first "Just Do It" ad aired on July 1, 1988, featuring Walt Stack, an 80-year-old marathon runner, jogging across San Francisco's Golden Gate Bridge. The narrative served as a thunderous slam dunk to Michael Jordan's iconic commercials, featuring Spike Lee as Mars Blackmon asking: "Is it the shoes?"

From the "Bo Knows" series starring multi-sport athlete Bo Jackson to the social justice stand initiated by former 49ers quarterback Colin Kaepernick, "Just Do It" has been the timeless narrative that unifies and connects five decades of brand storytelling. The "You Can't Stop Us" campaign from 2020 was not only appreciated for its inspirational message during the pandemic, it also reflected how the Nike brand has remained relevant, distinctive and adaptable. According to Jerome Conlon, Nike's director of brand planning at the time, "Just Do It" represented a major turning point, with sales increasing by 1000% over the next decade.

Author of the 2015 bestseller *Soulful Branding*, Conlon claims the narrative gave Nike poetic license to embrace and elevate its role as a spiritually charged brand. As Conlon explains, "People started reading things into it, much more than sport." Over time, Nike began receiving letters from people all over the country telling them how three simple, personally significant words inspired them to make epic changes to their lives by becoming more active.

From its co-founder's early experiences in World War II and its own humble beginnings as a small business start-up in 1964, Nike demonstrates a universal truth about how the greatest brands in history are created. And it is this:

Building a legendary brand only happens from the inside out.

True significance is only achieved when the core leadership of any company models their values on a daily basis. The tightly knit bond between Bill Bowerman and Phil Knight ensured that no one inside the company could miss seeing the virtues of courage, determination and ingenuity they brought to the business table. That unrelenting drive to play to win was baked into the company's cultural DNA in much the same manner as Bill Bowerman developed new shoe designs. But the branding stars began to align at outerspace levels when Nike started telling that three-word story that spoke to the human values that defined who they already were—beyond their products and services. Lyrically, poetically and commercially, this narrative tapped into the cultural zeitgeist by advancing a simple idea that transcended what Nike manufactured, shipped and sold.

Massive global success did not come about, however, simply because Nike adopted "Just Do It" or stamped a "swoosh" on their shoes. It's what the company actually *did* in terms of everyday behaviors and execution that gave the brand the horsepower to surpass mighty adversaries like Adidas and Puma. In other words, the narrative distilled an existing emotional truth. Like the Carolina Panthers, Nike simply told a story that was already theirs to begin with.

That's precisely what happened in the mid '80s when legendary Texas ad man Tim McClure developed a four-word battle cry that became the most successful anti-littering campaign in history. Working with the Texas Department of Transportation, McClure's short, double- entendre narrative spoke to the already healthy amount of Texan bravado, especially among the 18-to-35-year-old males most likely to litter. Being a true, red-white-and-blue Texan is often associated with a deep love affair with pick-up trucks, country music, shotguns, football and the Good Lord above—not necessarily in that order. The first 30-second spot for "Don't Mess With Texas" aired during the 1986 Cotton Bowl telecast featuring late bluesman Stevie Ray Vaughan. Since then, McClure's award-winning campaign has starred a number of iconic Texans, like Willie Nelson, the Dallas Cowboys, George Strait, LeAnn Rimes and Matthew McConaughey. The story they keep telling resonates with their target audience of "good ole boys" in such a way that a non-offensive, non-dramatic message like "Keep Texas Beautiful" never could.

Jim Gilbert recalls how his own father spent a tough and lonely childhood being shuttled between about 20 orphanages and foster homes before a French-speaking family based in Quebec City finally took him in. Jim remembers his dad repeatedly telling him, "You always have to be nice to people, even when they can't do anything in return." The values of caring, kindness, family and generosity were firmly embedded in Jim—and in Dawna, too—long before they discovered how a well-crafted Tribal Narrative would serve a broader, more meaningful purpose than just sales and marketing. For Canada's Huggable Car Dealer, it became a decision-making filter. The lens through which leaders at the dealership see the world, their place in it and the overarching idea that impacts everything from hiring to customer care, community involvement, social media presence and cultural alignment. More than anything, the "Huggable" narrative represents a bold leadership decision made by Jim and Dawna to stand in their own truth and be okay with letting the world know who they were—beyond four wheels and a piece of tin.

Remember our fictional insurance company, Jones & Smith? What if they had made a bold decision to stand out? What if they chose to *zag* away from all other providers and express who they really were as people—beyond the insurance policies they sell? What would it look and sound like if Jones & Smith communicated their character, ideals and values in such a way that they would never be confused with any other firm within 500 miles?

Suppose you visited their company, got to know the owners, talked to some of their people and discovered that the principals who ran Jones & Smith were one of the following:

a) Avid golfers
b) Whiskey enthusiasts
c) Dog lovers

Assuming these leaders were hardcore in their passion for any of these pursuits, it would be more than possible to craft a personalized, powerful Tribal Narrative. In other words, they could replicate the same brand philosophies employed by Nike, Apple, Queen, the Carolina Panthers and Jim Gilbert's Wheels & Deals. Their firm's brand narrative could sound like this:

a) Jones & Smith Insurance: "Drive Equals Distance."
b) Jones & Smith Insurance: "Blend Protection to Perfection."
c) Jones & Smith Insurance: "Run with the Pack."

Whether any of these narratives suit your personal taste is not the point. What's important is the strategic advantage Jones & Smith could create by telling a completely different story, by swimming away from all the others treading water in the sea of similarity.

Granted, these may be simplistic examples. But they reveal how anyone with a smidgen of imagination and determination can find a story within themselves that speaks to something more than standard marketing lingo based on "products, services, features, advantages, benefits."

A soul-stirring narrative for your brand becomes possible when you decide to escape the category mosh pit and create substantial differentiation. When you dare to lead the pack, not follow it.

Two years after "Just Do It" was launched and Air Jordan took flight, Queen's Brian May was in the Windy City for a game between the Bulls and the Los Angeles Lakers.

Watching Michael Jordan and Magic Johnson dazzle the crowd at old Chicago Stadium, May heard a familiar "stomp, stomp, clap." An echo rumbling from 20,000 people rising and chanting as one. Stunned by the magnitude of this audience participation, he realized his two-minute masterpiece had turned into something much bigger.

Queen's anthem belongs to all of us.

Timeless Takeaways

#1. Implant a mental stop sign for the mind.

With distracted, twitchy consumers processing more than 5,000 messages a day, a two-to-six-word Tribal Narrative gives you the chance to make them stop for a moment. Make them focus. Suddenly, they're paying attention, noticing something surprising, intriguing, inspiring and fascinating. Something comedic, delightful or enchanting. Regardless of the approach, it's crucial to make your potential customer slam on their mental brakes and give you a second look. Job #1 for any leader is to have a readily understood, showstopping phrase that increases the odds of standing out, getting shared and being remembered.

It doesn't matter whether you're selling computers, running shoes, or used cars, or even cleaning up Texas highways—creating a powerful brand narrative ultimately depends on the moral convictions of its leader. In the attention economy, your brand has microseconds to get noticed. You can't afford to be forgettable. Too much rides on this horse.

#2. Music and drama rock hearts and souls.

Storytelling and rhythmic sound is the perfect mix for speaking to human emotions. Ditch the plain-as-dishwater, cookie-cutter clichés you'll find all over your category. Draw your inspiration from poets, songwriters, filmmakers, novelists and other artists to create an original two-to-six-word narrative that mirrors who you really are—beyond the products or services you offer. Hunt underneath old rocks, like

Batman comic books, *Vogue* magazines or a collection of old Led Zeppelin cassettes to uncover ideas that speak your truth.

Brian May was inspired by the raucous singing and chanting of the Liverpool F.C. anthem "You'll Never Walk Alone." He went to sleep and woke up with "We Will Rock You" banging in his head. Apple's iconic "Here's to the Crazy Ones" was inspired by a scene from *Dead Poets Society*. Creative writing techniques such as alliteration, onomatopoeia or rhyming can be employed to craft a memorable catchphrase that melts like warm molasses in the mind of the market.

#3. When you get your story straight, it has no expiry date.

The future of your company depends on this. When the late Steve Jobs returned to a floundering Apple in 1997, it was hemorrhaging gallons of red ink. The company was in a death spiral. Vultures were circling. Without the leadership of Jobs, there's zero chance that a brand narrative as monstrously impactful as "Think Different" would have ever seen the light of day.

Cynically speaking, Apple's new brand strategy was a stalling tactic. With new, innovative products like the iMac at least a year away, shareholders and customers needed convincing that things would be different with Jobs back at the helm. Within six weeks of the first 60-second ad—broadcast September 28, 1997, on the network television premiere of *Toy Story*—Apple's share price had risen by more than 30%. Within 12 months, the stock tripled, despite having no significant new products to bring to the market. In effect, Apple was saved by a narrative—one that still speaks to the company's soul today.

Final Encore

Like any great rock anthem, Tribal Narratives have elements of elasticity. They stay relevant because their meaning changes over time, without being boxed in by the limited confines of a product or service. This is not an easy thing for a leader to discover. It demands a certain amount of soul-searching, maybe even outside professional help that offers different perspectives. Capturing the essence of your brand in a dramatic two-to-six-word phrase may be a little demanding, but any legend knows that nothing good comes easy.

Besides increase in revenues, market share, reputational equity and other measurable results experienced by Nike, Apple, the Carolina Panthers, the state of Texas or a Big Little Legend like Jim Gilbert, there's a lot for any leader to consider when weighing strategic options.

The cultural impact of a Tribal Narrative also extends far beyond any financial ROI. Real return lies in higher levels of alignment and engagement with your team and the genuine way people wear the heart of your brand on their sleeve. Tribal Narratives such as "Just Do It" or "Canada's Huggable Car Dealer" possess an uplifting human energy that transcends marketing while making a clear statement about your beliefs and values.

Can you metaphorically shift your focus from your products or services and concentrate instead on bigger, more inherently dramatic ideas to separate your brand from all the competitors in your region? Never forget: the goal is to break out, not blend in. To stand apart from 35,000 other paintings in the metaphorical Louvre of your category.

Don't ask if your dream to build a legendary brand is crazy.

Ask if that dream is crazy enough.

If you had invested $1,000 at Nike's 1980 IPO, your stock would be worth $52.15 million as of October 2019. That's a 5,215,378% rate of return, driven by the shared vision of two Oregon guys who refused to surrender.

Two guys who kept pounding.

Just did it.

And found their own way to rock.

It doesn't matter how many people you offend, as long as you're getting your message to your consumers. I say to those who do not want to offend anybody: You are going to have a very, very difficult time having meaningful advertising.

PHIL KNIGHT

8

WHISKEY BOTTLES AND OPEN-AIR WEDDINGS

How Symbols and Rituals Recruit and Rally Your Pack

April 23, 2005

When defeated French emperor Napoleon Bonaparte was being transported into exile on the island of Saint Helena, he told a British naval captain that "a soldier will fight long and hard and even die for a bit of colored ribbon." Later that same century, esteemed American essayist and philosopher Henry David Thoreau observed, "Live your beliefs and you can turn the world around."

Both Thoreau and Napoleon—from entirely different disciplines and different sides of the Atlantic Ocean—recognized a timeless truth that still drives people today.

What is the metaphorical equivalent to the colored piece of ribbon that represents your iron-clad beliefs and determines your behavior? Is there one symbolic icon or treasure that means so much to you that you would run back into a burning building to retrieve it?

As far back as 1815, Napoleon was sharing a key leadership tool confirmed and endorsed by Thoreau: Tangible Symbols and, by extension, Intangible Rituals. These two principles are indispensable for any leader who hopes to attract a purposeful group of like-minded people. Since the early 2000s and the information explosion detonated by the internet, symbols and rituals have proven resilient in breaking through brain clutter in a way language cannot. Prior to the written word, human groups used symbols to share thoughts, ideas and concepts. Organized religions employed symbols such as the crucifix or a stylized Buddha to connect with followers. Entire nations followed suit and began adopting flags, with Denmark earning the distinction of having the oldest flag still in use, dating back to 1219. For any leader who aspires to rally people and motivate them to commit to a cause bigger than themselves, Tangible Symbols and Intangible Rituals will never be a passing fad.

Never mind Napoleon and Thoreau.

Nobody knew this better than Jack.

The House That Jack Built

Jack was the youngest of ten kids. After his mother passed away during childbirth, he acquired three more siblings, along with a cantankerous stepmother. Then, things got much worse. While the Civil War raged all around them, Jack's father fell ill and died of pneumonia. With his older brothers off fighting for the Confederates, a rebellious teenage Jack up and ran away from home. He had but $9 in his pocket.

Jack found work on a farm owned by a preacher and moonshine distiller who assigned the young orphan to labor alongside an enslaved man. Nathan "Nearest" Green took Jack under his wing and schooled the lad in the fine art of making real Tennessee whiskey. After emancipation,

Green stayed on. When the reverend sold the farm to Jack, he made Green master distiller—the first at an expanding company that soon relocated to nearby Lynchburg, Tennessee. That's when Jack purchased Cave Spring Hollow and its surrounding property for $2,148, using an inheritance from his father's estate—a small fortune at the time.

Standing only five-foot-two, Jack faced a lot of competitors in those early days. Intuitively, the boy distiller knew he had to separate his brand from the others in a distinguishing, original way. When a traveling glass salesman showed him a prototype square bottle in 1895, Jack realized he'd stumbled onto something big. On a practical level, square bottles were easier to package and transport. But they also made a bold, visual statement that matched Jack's own beliefs. The square-shaped bottles symbolized his commitment to high standards, fairness and integrity. They would reinforce Jack's reputation as a man known for being a "square shooter for his square dealings."

But Jack didn't stop there. Not long after his whiskey won a gold medal at the 1904 World's Fair in St. Louis, Jack introduced the defiant black-and-white label proclaiming "Old No. 7." The image added a little more mystique to a symbol now known for something much more intriguing than the charcoal-mellowed liquid elixir bottled in those distinctive square containers. Jack had laid an all-important foundation for a brand that began to build a sizeable fan base that included the likes of 1949 Nobel Prize winner William Faulkner and British prime minister Sir Winston Churchill.

By the mid-1950s, the little Tennessee company was still a small, regional brand, depending on organic word-of-mouth to sell about 150,000 cases a year. But, midway through the Eisenhower administration, sales began to take off and those numbers doubled. And began to climb, year after year. The Mona Lisa Effect had taken hold. Customer preference for the brand continues unabated to this day, with Jack Daniel's ranked #1 for whiskey sales in America and top five globally for wine and spirits.

What happened that tilted the competitive playing field so drastically? What single event stirred so much demand stateside for Jack Daniel's that it delayed international export of the product for almost two decades?

You can blame it on a single moment—say, sometime in the summer of 1955, when Frank's new best friend Jack was first poured into a glass in front of him at a Manhattan bar. Down on his luck, Frank Sinatra was venting out his lady troubles when his friend and fellow entertainer Jackie Gleason ordered him a shot of Jack Daniel's. Another version of the story asserts that Sinatra discovered Jack Daniel's Tennessee Whiskey through fellow film star and celebrity Humphrey Bogart. No matter how it really played out, once Frank had that first sip, he and Jack became inseparable—through four marriages, countless liaisons and many boozy all-nighters.

They went everywhere together. Especially on stage. One fateful night at a mid-'50s performance in Las Vegas, Sinatra took his Jack on the rocks with a splash of water, held it up before the crowd and uttered this blessing: "Ladies and gentlemen, this is Jack Daniel's, and it's the nectar of the gods." The line stuck. It was picked up by the press. The legendary crooner publicly endorsing his tipple of choice became a tipping point. Jack became a household name.

Now that the coolest guy in the room was drinking Jack, the multitudes wanted a sip for themselves. Sinatra loved Jack so much that he demanded a ready supply from each venue on his tours. In many ways, Sinatra was an early pioneer of influencer marketing. But he was never a hired shill. Never got paid a dime for endorsing the product. Without a contract, paycheck or royalties, Ol' Blue Eyes elevated Jack Daniel's from small, regional player to pop-culture icon.

When the bad boy from Hoboken, New Jersey, was hobnobbing with his Rat Pack friends, he often wore a blazer with a patch of two crossed golf clubs and a bottle, for the imaginary "Jack Daniel's Country Club." This authentic endorsement from the man who belted out "My Way" triggered a domino effect among generations of entertainers. You can see clear evidence of the Mona Lisa Effect in each photo of a rock star or celebrity hoisting an anti-establishment bottle of Old No. 7. The Rolling Stones, Led Zeppelin, Van Halen, Mötley Crüe, Slash, Lemmy, Ke$ha and numerous others have followed Sinatra. True to form, when he passed in 1998, the "Chairman of the Board" was buried with a pack of Camels and a bottle of Jack.

Jack Daniel's has always taken the matter of Strategic Drama very seriously—and anchored it with by Tangible Symbols and Intangible Rituals—but they really get your attention when they deliver that message directly to a front porch—in this case, mine. On November 17, 2013, a FedEx package arrived with two sealed documents. One was a cover letter and personal welcome from the managing director of Jack Daniel's, Mr. John V. Hayes, granting approval for membership in the world-famous Tennessee Squire

Association. The other document was an official deed and title that conveyed legal ownership of real estate in the County of Moore, Tennessee.

The elegant legalese of this deed and title informs the holder they are in possession of an "unrecorded" plot of land situated near Cave Springs Hollow, where Jack Daniel's whiskey is distilled to this day. According to the laws of the State of Tennessee, the actual property, with its confidential plot number, can be bequeathed to the holder's heirs upon their untimely demise. In our household, this deed and title has been hermetically sealed and locked away for posterity.

The Tennessee Squire Association dates back to an idea hatched in 1956 by the distiller's first national sales manager, Winton Smith. After Sinatra's public benedictions, demand for Jack Daniel's was flying to the moon and beyond. Production could not keep up. Purchasers were forced to wait. Feeling restless, Winton wanted to keep his customers happy while whetting their appetite in the interim. He decided that loyal fans who had written letters saying they could not get any Jack Daniel's would instead receive a designated plot of land—one square inch of unrecorded property on distillery grounds—legally making them part owners, or "Squires."

This one gesture of Abundant Generosity still reverberates to this day. Tennessee Squires all over the planet bond, ponder and pontificate about their preference for a libation born of pure limestone spring water. As Winton originally wrote in his first letter to the Squires, "It is just our feeling that too little time is spent in this day and age enjoying the friendship of others. This is our small attempt to speak up."

The official deed and title is an example of how a symbol can turn that intangible generous spirit into a tangible reality. Currently, 34,688 Tennessee Squires the world over share that love with others: an exclusive fraternity that would make both Jack and Frank proud. Through the Civil War, Prohibition, two world wars, Vietnam and the global pandemic of 2020, Jack Daniel's has relied on Tangible Symbols and Intangible Rituals to keep their story alive and kicking. The baseline symbol for any organization is its logo, often accompanied by "brand" colors with specific fonts, wordmarks and visual styles. But creating an irresistible force that inspires generational loyalty extends far beyond these basic elements of graphic design.

Symbols and the Subconscious Mind

Visualize an evergreen tree in your living room, decked out with twinkling lights and colorful ornaments. What holiday would you be thinking about? Which one of the four seasons comes to mind? Does the image make you think of a specific month and day?

If you were thinking about a) Christmas, b) winter and c) December 25, you just experienced what countless studies have confirmed. Symbolic thought affects subconscious thinking. In some cases, spoken or written words are completely unnecessary to convey a message. Without reason or rhyme, symbols are always ready for prime time.

These physical and visual signatures take many forms. They can be packaging differentiators, like Jack Daniel's square bottle or Apple's white box. Symbols can express luxury status, like French shoe designer Christian Louboutin and his high stiletto heels bearing a distinct shade of red called Pantone 18-1663 TPX. Often priced above $1,000 a pair, this footwear icon was inspired in part by Andy Warhol's *Flowers*. Louboutin's decision to use a "Chinese-red hue" turned an otherwise ordinary black shoe into a must-have on red carpets the world over. By the same token, symbols like Wisconsin's "Cheesehead," Pittsburgh's "Terrible Towel" or the watermelon headgear worn by rabid fans of the CFL's Saskatchewan Roughriders apply similar principles of symbolism to communicate powerful, unspoken messages.

Personal authenticity, integrity and independence are universal ideals symbolized by a square bottle of Old No. 7. Duty, honor and sacrifice are universal ideals symbolized by a shiny medal or a bright colored ribbon for which a soldier would be willing to lay down their life. People inside and outside your company thirst to rally around something bigger than a paycheck. When you supply a Tangible Symbol of something to believe in, they will go to the ends of the earth to protect what they see as sacred.

The late Steve Jobs used symbolic thought to communicate the value of Apple's Genius Bar and its battalions of brainiac techies. With images of Albert Einstein and Sir Isaac Newton floating through our subconscious, the use of the atomic symbol at any Genius Bar reinforces our belief that this is more than just another customer service help desk. Fictional or human symbols such as Colonel Sanders, Captain Crunch, Tony the Tiger, Mr. Clean, the Energizer Bunny, the Michelin Man or the Most Interesting Man in the

World have all cemented public recognition while bolstering the bottom line of the brands they represent. Each delivers a "gut feeling" in how we perceive products like athletic shoes, beer, batteries, breakfast cereal, fried chicken, headphones, underwear, fragrances, shampoos or soft drinks—especially when those products are endorsed by celebrities such as Michael Jordan, LeBron James, David Beckham, Jennifer Aniston, Charlize Theron or Beyoncé.

Like a secular religion, the wide world of sports also offers its own unique array of symbolic artifacts. Olympic gold medals, golf's Green Jacket, Super Bowl rings, championship belts, yellow jerseys, the Heisman Trophy and the Stanley Cup are examples of objects that have taken on epic and mythical qualities. Euphoric players and coaches become so jubilant over winning such coveted prizes that they'll drink from it, sleep with it or give that Holy Grail a big, slobbery kiss—no matter how unhygienic that may be.

These tangible entities are comparable to ancient amulets and talismans, endowed with enchanted, mystical energies that deliver special privileges and benefits to the possessor.

In the opening scene of *The Da Vinci Code*, the character Robert Langdon displays a number of symbols at a university lecture, asking students what they represent. Langdon explains how symbols transmit ideas whenever language and comprehension is a barrier. Prior to the introduction of Gutenberg's printing press in 1440, only kings, priests and the nobility had means and ability to read and write. For centuries, churches, monarchies and landowners relied heavily on symbols and imagery to control and communicate with the hoi polloi. The Star of David, the Union Jack, the Jolly Roger, the Confederate Stars and Bars, the Nazi swastika and the Pride Rainbow have all motivated people to march. The iconic image of American troops raising "Old Glory" on a Japanese island during World War II dramatically illustrates how a compelling symbol can drive everyday people to move mountains.

Nearly 7,000 Marines and naval personnel paid the ultimate price to capture a small volcanic island of great strategic importance. Twenty-seven Medals of Honor were awarded for acts of valor in the Battle of Iwo Jima, more than any other battle in U.S. history. In the middle of gruesome combat, AP photographer Joe Rosenthal captured the precise moment when five U.S. Marines and a Navy sailor raised the Stars and Stripes on the summit of Mount Suribachi—a frozen image that went viral.

The front-page photo unleashed waves of hope that victory in the Pacific was near. Millions were inspired to dig deeper, buy more war bonds and keep America's economy rolling. The most reproduced photograph in history helped hasten the end to all the bloodshed. Rosenthal's Pulitzer Prize–winning photograph has since become the unofficial symbol of the Marine Corps. The memorial statue in Arlington, Virginia, immortalizes this single photo, epitomizing the Marines' core values of bravery, sacrifice and teamwork. Any leader determined to create a larger-than-life brand is wise to pay close attention to these sword-in-the-stone, foundational concepts that have stood the test of time for centuries.

One of the best modern-day examples of how a Tangible Symbol can be synchronized with an Intangible Ritual is being lived out loud every single day at another Big Little

Legend: a tiny, yet tasteful wedding chapel nestled in the heart of the Lone Star State.

Her name is Chapel Dulcinea.

From Here to Texas . . . Till Death Do Us Part

More than a thousand times each year, couples from all over the world descend on Texas Hill Country to be wed in an elegant, open-air chapel perched on the edge of a small cliff. Constructed on an ancient Native American trail on the outskirts of Austin, Chapel Dulcinea was dedicated on April 23, 2005, coinciding with one of the most significant dates in the history of Western literature. Spain's most celebrated writer, Miguel de Cervantes, author of the magnum opus *Don Quixote*, laid down his pen and entered the pearly gates on April 23, 1616. That same day, the most revered author in the history of the English language, Sir William Shakespeare, joined him in the heavens. Two great voices silenced on the same sundown.

The impact from their prodigious quills will be felt for eternity. While Shakespeare authored many classics, including the tragic love story of Romeo and Juliet, Cervantes produced the second most translated work in history after the Bible. Often considered the first modern novel, the majestic and noble tale of Don Quixote is punctuated by a romantic quest for the hand and heart of the feminine ideal. Symbolically, Dulcinea represents the impossible dream. She is the archetype of perfection to be admired only from afar. Unreachable. Unattainable.

In the eyes of the admirer, Dulcinea is comparable to
Charlie Brown's Little Red-Haired Girl. For lovestruck
prankster salesman Jim Halpert at Dunder Mifflin paper
company in Scranton, Pennsylvania, she is shy, artistically
inclined receptionist Pam Beesly. Don Quixote sees Dulcinea as the most perfect woman on earth. He sees himself
as her white knight and worthy champion. Once she says yes
to a proposal, the engagement will be followed by a ritual
that bonds their hearts and unites the couple for eternity.

Few human experiences offer such a vast, varied and
consistent menu of rituals like the wedding ceremony. Best
men and maids of honor. Readings of scripture. The bride's
slow processional walk down the aisle. An exchange of vows
followed by a pronouncement from a third-party authority
figure before the union is sealed with a kiss. As they depart,
the couple is showered with rice or petals from well-wishers,
then they all gather at a reception featuring multiple
speeches of welcome, the newlyweds' first waltz, a pristine
wedding cake and intoxicated relatives busting their best
dance-floor moves.

None of that pomp and circumstance happened for a
young couple of humble means from Broken Arrow, Okla-
homa. Roy and Pennie attended the Sweetheart Banquet
when they were both 14. Four years later, they went to the
high school prom together. Dropping out of college after
only two days, Roy thought it was the perfect moment to
get hitched with his princess. Two crazy kids living on love
and buying on time from a one-bedroom apartment.

Today, after more than 40 years of marriage with two
sons, grandchildren and never-ending daily adventures of

building a world-class business, Roy and Pennie Williams have always known that the #1 secret to success in business and in life is making a commitment to someone other than yourself. In the late 1990s, Roy wrote a trilogy of bestselling business books, establishing him as America's top advertising expert. After relocating to Austin, the Williamses began planning a 30-acre campus for a business school called Wizard Academy. Breaking ground on January 1, 2005, the construction of their first building—Chapel Dulcinea—demonstrated how Roy and Pennie planted their own flag of commitment to give couples all over the world the wedding they never had.

Without regard to family background or financial circumstances.

Absolutely free of charge—no strings attached—anyone can be joined in holy matrimony at Chapel Dulcinea. Couples have traveled from as far away as Australia, Belarus, Bermuda, Canada, Denmark, Germany, Japan, Kenya, Norway, Slovenia and New Zealand, all pulled toward Texas by the magnetic qualities of a Big Little Legend.

All societies engage in Intangible Rituals. Everything from religious worship to rites of passage, and from oaths of allegiance to coronations, presidential inaugurations, bootcamp initiations and more. Military salutes or the French custom of a kiss on both cheeks are forms of rituals. Baptism ceremonies, bar mitzvahs, debutante balls, funeral wakes, graduations and countless birthday parties—all of the truly important moments of our lives revolve around ritualistic events that signify our personal biographies.

You will discover a dizzying array of such activities in the wide world of sports. The lighting of the Olympic Flame. Pre-game tailgating. Detroit hockey fans who toss octopuses at Red Wings games. Playoff beards and face-painting (like New Jersey Devils fan David Puddy on *Seinfeld*) are traditions embraced by millions of athletes and fans. The Lambeau Leap. Drinking milk after winning the Indy 500. Strawberries and cream at Wimbledon. English soccer fan singalongs. The Yankees blasting Sinatra's "New York, New York" after every home victory or the post-series handshake lineups after each round of the Stanley Cup playoffs.

For Whom the Bell Tolls

Together, Wizard Academy and Chapel Dulcinea provide any visitor with a rare example of how symbols and rituals can come together to create a feeling of divine enchantment. Everything is done with intention. Starting with stylish Spanish architecture, Chapel Dulcinea has 12 upper windows that speak of 12 months, 12 tribes of Israel and 12 apostles of Jesus. Once inside the chapel, you can look up and observe the timber of the roof's interior, made to resemble the belly of the whale from the story of Jonah, who repented and got a second chance.

After saying "I do," the bride and groom take a symbolic walk out to the edge of a daunting cliff to symbolize their mutual leap of faith. Inside the chapel stands a 160-year-old oak door that leads to a bell tower, where the newly married couple joins hands to ring the 1882 bronze church bell and announce their union to the world. Tripadvisor is flooded with reviews that speak of breathtaking views, tasteful, rustic themes and an intimate, natural setting.

After nightfall, wander over to the Wizard's Tower and behold another sturdy symbol of commitment. On the tower rooftop stands an Excalibur-like sword in a stone located on the south wall. When night falls, you can easily see that the tip of the sword touches the North Star, that celestial beacon of hope and fixed navigational landmark that sailors have depended on for centuries. It's the perfect metaphor for any navigator on the ocean of life seeking a purposeful destination. And when the lights go down, Wizard Academy students take the traditional "Tour of Scotland," where whisky sommelier Daniel Whittington introduces five regions of single malt scotch. Hosted at the Toad & Ostrich pub, it offers guests samples of some of Scotland's finest spirits from one of the most diverse whisky collections in Texas. The sprawling campus is also adorned with many statues and artistic tributes to Hemingway, Picasso, Steinbeck and others, adding deeply symbolic layers to create a modern-day mythology.

Tangible Symbols and Intangible Rituals are not the exclusive, private domain of world-class brands like Jack Daniel's, Apple, the Olympic Games, the Marine Corps or Chapel Dulcinea. Any leader from any industry or category can apply this unorthodox yet effective approach, including a business-to-business environment. With head offices in Edmonton, Alberta, Raptor Mining has drilled deep into the exploration of minerals and natural resources, as well as of symbols and rituals. CEO Craig Harder is on a mission to create a shared spirit of initiative and unity among his 300-plus employees spread across distant locations. With more than 70 patents and a global partnership with Caterpillar, Raptor Mining provides highly specialized industrial parts for mining, dredging, power generation and construction in more than 175 countries. But creating an aligned workplace culture spanning several continents is never an easy feat.

Things got serious in 2015 when Craig introduced Raptor's official motto, expressed with the patented, double-entendre acronym GSD. On the one hand, the GSD narrative speaks to the need for "goal-setting discussions" in areas such as new product designs, robotics or strengthening customer relationships. The other is to "get s**t done." Both philosophies have been around since Raptor's inception, but GSD took on a life of its own when the company created symbolic stickers and swag that employees could place on phones, notebooks and toolboxes. Wander through their offices and you'll see nearly every desk festooned with bright orange GSD buttons that deliver a voice-activated response when pushed.

Craig also has a reptilian alter ego, donning a full-colored dinosaur mask for company videos, Facebook Live streams and Instagram posts. Known as the Raptor CMO, this pre-historic character resonates with anyone who interacts with the company, like the time it earned Craig the rock star treatment on a visit to a CAT factory in Johannesburg, South Africa. From more than 15,000 miles away, Craig's hosts could not believe that the CEO of a company would go to such lengths to stand out. It was in that moment that

Craig grasped the widespread appeal and clout of the Raptor brand, and its impact on increasing sales, customer acquisition and deepening relationships.

Reflecting on his company's core values of productivity, simplicity and velocity while having fun, Craig acknowledges that Raptor Mining has made great use of symbols and rituals to connect in a powerful, provocative and playful manner with their team and their customers. Building a positive and magnetically attractive culture with annual multi-day events like RaptorFest is something Craig takes seriously. As this dinosaur-mask wearing father of two puts it, "Our GSD culture is the driving force of our value proposition. GSD stands for getting s**t done, and it helps to have symbols that express that."

When that FedEx package first arrived on my doorstep in 2013, it uncorked with stunning clarity how few weapons in any leader's arsenal are more formidable than symbols and rituals. Aspirational brands like Jack Daniel's—along with Apple, Chapel Dulcinea and Raptor Mining—represent much more below the surface of their products and services.

The fusing of bedrock values with symbols and rituals to form lasting bonds may explain why fictional branch manager Michael Scott dedicates so much of his valuable executive time to planning his annual company awards show, the Dundies.

Timeless Takeaways

#1. Be an amateur anthropologist.

The study of anthropology—analyzing human norms, values, languages, cultures and economies—helps us understand past and present societies. Whether it's a school marching band, Little League team, military unit, nation, church or brand, start by asking why certain symbols and rituals stand the test of time. What underlying dynamics help an individual identify with the group? Why do those same forces exclude those who don't feel they belong?

Long-term brand building is where the disciplines of business and cultural sociology intersect. Harley fans are less concerned with product specifics such as torque generation or multi-point fuel injection systems. They care much more about the human values of freedom, rebellion and a love for the open road—to the point where many seal that allegiance by wearing a tattoo of the company's logo.

#2. Swim through subconscious waters.

You don't have to be Sigmund Freud to know that humans are strange beings. Often saying one thing. Doing another.

An Austrian neurologist and the controversial founder of psychoanalysis, Freud described the human brain as an iceberg, with the deepest part—our subconscious—as the 90% resting below the surface. Dominated by survival instincts and primal emotions, our subconscious plays a key role in our conscious buying behaviors, such as choosing a particular brand of whiskey or welding tool, a certain laundry detergent, car dealer, coffee shop, razor blade, burger joint, motorcycle or wedding venue.

Tangible Symbols and Intangible Rituals play a vital role in making this neurological joyride a little smoother. This is why mascots and symbols like teddy bears can be essential if your brand needs to address deeply rooted trust issues in a category like used cars. At Canada's Huggable Car Dealer, customers enjoy both the physical and virtual exchange of "the hug" as well as the opportunity to name a giant teddy bear with every vehicle purchase via an official digital ceremony. Since the days of Napoleon, visionary leaders like Jim and Dawna Gilbert have paid close attention to the subconscious thinking that drives buying behavior.

#3. Convert attention into attachment.

People don't bond with faceless corporations. They only form emotional attachments with brands that reflect human qualities and values.

Once a brand story attracts initial attention in the marketplace, visionary leaders will want to build enduring relationships through the wordless language of symbols and rituals. When relationships are shallow and transactional to begin with, it becomes a weary uphill battle toward growth and profitability. Companies that fail to develop strong ties with their customers and employees experience more churn and turnover. Their survival depends on short-term discounting and cost-cutting before the inevitable death spiral toward lower profit margins. What steps will you take to invest in your brand and inspire the equivalent to an Apple decal on somebody's car, or a GSD button on their desk?

How About a Nightcap?

Tangible Symbols and Intangible Rituals are a break from the humdrum of everyday life. They reduce complexity and provide context in a sometimes confusing world. They also tackle the isolation of the digital age, and the growing need among people to seek more than just superficial online connections.

The doorway to the customer's subconscious mind is open to those brave enough to venture inward. Are there elements of your brand story that could be distilled and expressed through ritualistic actions or symbolic shorthand? Do you have clarity on your Mount Suribachi of values, beliefs and ideals you are willing to die for? Can you start thinking of potential symbolic flags you could fly to state and enshrine those beliefs, and consistent rituals that could reinforce and defend those values?

Big Little Legends are created with noble intent from the inside out by purpose-driven leaders who recognize how symbols and rituals support worthy intentions. Aimless is the man, woman, nation or brand that has no symbols or rituals. Careless are those who choose their meaning without great consideration.

Tangible Symbols and Intangible Rituals welcome others to our clan. They allow them to be an insider in our select, private club.

And enjoy the party with new friends like Frank and Jack.

One man, scorned and covered with scars,

still strove with his last ounce of courage

to reach the unreachable stars;

and the world was better for this.

MIGUEL DE CERVANTES

9

___

BRAVE THE NEW BRAND WORLD

Why You Need to Become Your Own Media Company

April 9, 2012

Grade 10 was a tough year for Casey.

He and Robin were barely scraping by in their Connecticut trailer park.

He had a part-time dishwashing job at a touristy seafood restaurant.

Robin was pregnant. Casey was only 16.

The struggles for this young couple were all too real. Social assistance and a promotion to short-order fry cook helped, but not enough.

No matter how hard they tried, Casey and Robin couldn't get on the proverbial "same page" as partners or parents. Forced to drop out of school, Casey took custody of two-year-old Owen and headed for the concrete jungle of New York City. With no education, no job prospects and nothing left to lose, he showed up in the Big Apple with a toddler, a camcorder, $800 in his pocket and all his earthly possessions packed into a single duffle bag.

Once settled in Midtown Manhattan, he discovered his passion for filmmaking. In his spare time between bike messenger gigs, Casey started filming everything and anything. Burned the camcorder at both ends. Started making movies nonstop. With no friends, no social life and a young child to take care of, he spent his evenings editing on an iMac. Learning his craft. Sharpening his ability to attract eyeballs.

Casey's first big break came in 2003, with a three-minute home movie called *iPod's Dirty Secret*. Within a month, it was viewed by more than 6 million people. The *Washington Post* wrote an article—coining the phrase "viral video"—and soon his story was being shared by mainstream media outlets the world over, including the BBC, CNN, Fox News, NBC and Al Jazeera. Back in 2003, going viral was a big deal. Social media hadn't been invented yet. Two years before the launch of Facebook, Twitter and YouTube, Casey had found a way to attract attention.

His next big break came in June 2011, when a beef with the local constabulary and "stupid" bylaws prompted him to upload another three-minute video that cost $40 to produce. After receiving a ticket from the NYPD for riding his bike outside designated bike lanes, Casey created a mockingly hilarious video that lampooned the rigid letter of that law. He pedaled along marked lanes, allowing himself to crash into anything blocking his path, including construction barriers, delivery trucks and a police car. At a time when YouTube was in its infancy, "Bike Lanes" generated 5 million views the first day. Another 5 million the next day. On the third day, New York mayor Michael Bloomberg was being grilled for answers about the video at a packed press conference. A few days later, Casey got a call from the *New York Times* asking if he could make videos for them.

On a shoestring budget with no formal training, Casey Neistat had become a self-made professional videographer with a proven track record for getting people to drop what they're doing and pay attention. Soon he was fielding requests from companies all over America asking if he could do the same thing for them. One of those calls had an Oregon area code.

A marketing exec from Nike was on the line, asking if he could produce three online videos for their new Fuelband fitness tracker. After making the first two ads, Casey felt a little boxed in. Chafing at the creative restrictions from the world's biggest athletic brand, Casey threw away the script for the third and final video. Together, he and editor Max Joseph took the remaining $25,000 budget and, with no plan or premeditation, said "f**k it." They grabbed backpacks, headed to the airport and left the country.

Nothing they created resembled any traditional ad. Casey and Max had spent ten days shooting the world's most expensive travel journal. A voyage of 34,000 miles across three continents, 13 countries and 16 cities, including Bangkok, Paris, London and Nairobi. Two buddies on a breathtaking adventure, making every second count until the money runs out. They captured 29 hours of footage—including a gripping, slow-motion leap off a ridiculously high cliff in Oman.

Once back in NYC, the duo had 11 days to deliver a finished product. They had no clue how the Nike suits would feel about their act of creative rebellion. Would their corporate patrons approve? Would they be okay with how Casey and his trusty travel sidekick spent their money?

On April 9, 2012, the riveting 4:38 account of their global escapade was uploaded to YouTube.

In less than 72 hours, "Make It Count" racked up 1.5 million views. By the end of the week, it surpassed the 3 million mark.

For years, it was Nike's most viewed ad. By the end of 2020 it had topped 30 million views. It has been frequently lauded as the best brand story ever told on the internet. Casey's whirlwind trek kicked the Mona Lisa Effect into high gear, cementing his legacy as one of the most influential YouTubers of all time. A teen welfare dad had become an international media icon. "Make It Count" may not have been what Nike was expecting as a finished product, but it received truckloads of attention that no regular TV spot could ever hope to attract.

As Casey explains in the video, "Life is either daring adventure or nothing at all." In total, he has cranked out more than a thousand YouTube videos. Entering 2021, his audience had swelled to more than 12 million subscribers, generating in excess of 3 billion views. His incredible rags-to-riches rise as an online personality, vlogger, filmmaker and entrepreneur has accumulated a net worth of $12 million and a reputation as a global authority on new media.

So how does a guy with a $150 webcam get millions of views while traditional media outlets struggle to get a few thousand?

It's a story that needed to be explained to me.

When Casey Came Home for Christmas

The smoke had cleared. The dust had settled. Another Christmas season was in the books. The tree was still standing. Presents had been put away and all nattering relatives had departed. Relaxing over evening tumblers of holiday cheer, Dana and I were confronted with insistent urgings from her then-17-year-old son Josh to look at this strange, slightly offbeat, energetic YouTube character. Obliging the persistent teenager, we watched six or seven videos of a dude with wild curly hair in ripped jeans, T-shirt and funky sunglasses skateboarding or bicycling through New York City. We had no idea who he was or what we were really watching.

While the videos were visually compelling, with arresting time lapses of some of the coolest scenery in the world, we could not understand the point of it all. Why would nonsensical, juvenile videos from this Casey guy matter to anyone—especially in the business world? How would you monetize this? How could this approach help sell something or build a brand? Politely, we feigned interest in this latest teenage fixation, but internally blew Casey off as a waste of time. Meanwhile, Josh was breathlessly telling us of his addiction to the short vlogs that this animated New Yorker has been posting daily since March 2015.

Can you recall certain moments in your life when you were forced to look into a mirror and see something you didn't like a whole lot?

What happened the next day in our festive home will remind you of that famous scene out of *Moneyball*, when Billy Beane, played by Brad Pitt, attempts in vain to show a long-in-the-tooth Oakland A's scouting staff the future of player evaluation and development. Unwilling to let the debate end, Josh begged and pleaded with us to watch one more video. Reluctantly, we stared into his laptop screen once again—only this time, Josh clicked on the "Make It Count" masterpiece. The same one with financial backing from the brand known for its "swoosh."

Within the first 30 seconds, I came face-to-face with the real idiot in the room. It was that metaphorical smack-in-the-face when you suddenly realize you've been asking the wrong questions.

> Josh, do you mean to tell us that Nike is paying sunglasses dude real money to run around with a video camera and tell stories like this? And the reason Nike is doing this is that they see how the value dynamics of marketing have completely shifted? How many millions of views did this thing get? Did everything we thought we knew about marketing and advertising for decades just get flipped upside down?

That's the honest-to-goodness, real-life story of how an older, white suburban boomer began to grasp the strategic significance of what Casey Neistat was really doing. How this Big Little Legend was disrupting the art and science of brand building in the brave new world of social media.

He wasn't *renting* the audience. He was *building and owning* the audience. Without having to pay media gatekeepers.

Besides Nike, Casey has been involved in digital video projects for brands like Mercedes-Benz, J.Crew, Samsung and Google. On the weekend we "met," Casey had accumulated over a billion views, with a subscriber list of 2.2 million. While the numbers have skyrocketed since then, it was clear to see he had already acquired *the* most valuable asset for any leader who aspires to build an irresistible brand. In the middle of a noisy world, he organically grew an enraptured audience that paid complete attention. Without paid advertising budgets or mainstream media, Casey Neistat became the sole owner of a sizeable, loyal and fervently passionate audience growing every single second of every YouTube minute, hour and day. Owned it lock, stock and two smoking barrels.

Casey's success story forces any leader to start asking entirely new questions about modern-day brand building. Since the advent of social media, traditional marketers and media platforms have waged many a campaign against the winds of change. While mass populations of ears and eyeballs abandoned platforms like newspapers, radio stations, magazines or Yellow Pages, owners of those outlets kept fighting the disruption, much like power barons in the music industry who fought a losing battle to maintain bricks-and-mortar retail over streaming services. When something no longer works, you can be dead certain a sizeable number of status quo fuddy-duddies will try to keep it alive.

Hockey great Wayne Gretzky said, "Skate to where the puck is going to be, not to where it has been." Just as Gretzky articulates how the gift of anticipating the future helped him become the most prolific scorer in the history of his sport, another illustrious Canuck smiles from above, nodding his scholarly head in full agreement.

Marshall and His Message

Philosopher, communications theorist and academic rebel Marshall McLuhan became internationally famous in the 1960s for his studies on how mass media affects thought and human behavior.

This deeply literate, pipe-smoking Canadian has been compared to Darwin and Freud for the universal significance of his work. It was McLuhan who coined expressions such as "the medium is the message" and "the global village." He predicted the advent of the internet and virtual reality as early as 1964. Often mocked and derided by intellectual guardians of his day, McLuhan's theories are now being viewed as more relevant now than when he was alive.

McLuhan contended that the progress of any society can be tied to the rise of a specific technology or platform during that period: from the printing press, telegraph and telephone to newspapers, radio, motion pictures, television and now the internet. According to McLuhan, all content acts on human senses and reshapes sensory balance, which in turn has the power to reshape entire societies. The iPhone is just one example of how new technology created a user-driven, participatory culture, where content is produced, uploaded, converged, debated and reconstructed. This is what McLuhan had in mind when he described the global village as a place where "humans will always be connected by continuous and instantaneous electronic media."

McLuhan's insights reveal how marketers have always needed to adapt to the communication platforms of the day.

If William Shakespeare, Samuel Morse, Alexander Graham Bell, Thomas Edison, Guglielmo Marconi, Amelia Earhart, Winston Churchill and Marilyn Monroe were alive today, they would be perfecting their social media skills while planning their next TED Talk or Netflix original.

Watching the "Make It Count" video was like attending a crash course on the value of media literacy. It was the foreshadowing of why digital fluency matters in the 21st century. As McLuhan elegantly pointed out, history reveals that media are man-made constructions that evolve over time. The impact of the content depends to a large degree on the nature of the medium and how audiences draw meaning from the content on their own terms.

As a recovering broadcast journalist, my personal and professional experience on this subject was formed through a two-decade career in the 1980s and '90s with gigs in towns like Red Deer, Calgary and my hometown of Moncton, New Brunswick. I held more than 30,000 on-air appearances; 10,000-plus interviews with newsmakers, celebrities and athletes; event coverage that ranged from city hall meetings to political rallies, murder trials and 1,000-plus games of pro hockey play-by-play with minor-league affiliates of the Edmonton Oilers, Calgary Flames and Winnipeg Jets. As a foot soldier in the information wars waged through 20th-century broadcast studios, I engaged in hand-to-hand delivery, reporting on triumphs and tragedies of others and chronicling great moments and bitter defeats while employed by media companies profiting from those stories. We who inhabited those newsrooms were the unfettered gatekeepers of all public information deemed worthy to share, and the corporate chieftains who controlled those outlets owned their audiences, and then sold them to advertisers who had money to burn.

Companies who bought ads and sponsored shows in that era paid a handsome ransom for rented audiences. Starting from the *Mad Men* era of the 1950s, this message distribution strategy worked its magic like a box of Lucky Charms on Captain Crunch steroids. The factory model of traditional media conducted business in an undisturbed manner for nearly seven decades. The more people they interrupted with their commercials, the more products they sold, unleashing a vicious cycle of more ads to interrupt more people, more frequently. Swarms of lookalike companies began pitching average products for average masses of people. It's hardly surprising that these dynamics shaped core curriculum at business schools everywhere, with students drilled on the classic "4 Ps of Marketing": product, price, promotion and placement. First published in 1960, the "4 Ps" emerged as the dominant framework for marketing management decisions, guaranteeing that graduates would repeat this intellectual cycle 10 million times over.

If everyone goes to the same business schools learning the same ideas from the same professors, is it a shock to see so many people in the business world thinking the same way?

When the web was still finding its footing around the turn of the century, there were distant early warnings about an entirely new and different way of marketing. Some of those faint initial signals were beaming in from one-man radar stations like Casey Neistat who recognized the advantage of bypassing traditional media hierarchies to share knowledge with blinding speed. Once consumers were in control, long-term brand building shifted forever from a one-way interruption to a two-way conversation.

Ben Franklin and a Whole New Ballgame

Marketing strategies employed by a founding father from Philadelphia, a modern-day energy drink and a minor-league baseball team can help any business leader bridge centuries of understanding. There is really nothing new about "content marketing." The practice dates back more than 300 years, back to when Benjamin Franklin was trying to find customers for his printing business.

Besides being a businessman, diplomat, scientist, inventor, author, political philosopher, musician, postmaster, civil servant and kite enthusiast, Ben Franklin is considered to be the original content marketer. When he published the inaugural edition of *Poor Richard's Almanack* on December 28, 1732, Franklin offered his readers collections of poems, observations, weather, prose and sayings that indirectly promoted his printing services. In effect, he created a mental version of the Trojan horse: entering the mind of the consumer and giving them a reason to engage. Naturally, his shop snuck into their top-of-mind awareness, ready to leap forward whenever they required printing services. Franklin published *Poor Richard's Almanack* for 25 years, selling more than 10,000 copies annually and cementing his legacy as one of history's all-time thought leaders.

Fast-forward to 1895. Printing presses and distribution methods have become more efficient. And John Deere plunged into the content marketing deep end with *The Furrow*. For farmers, it was the agrarian equivalent to *Rolling Stone*. Popularity of the magazine snowballed, with circulation reaching 4 million at its peak in 1912. Still widely read today, *The Furrow* is now led by a six-person content team that editor David Jones describes as the "Led Zeppelin of agricultural journalism."

Five years after John Deere dipped their toes into the content marketing waters, Andre and Edouard Michelin published their first-ever road guide. In 1900 there were only 3,000 cars in France. The Michelin brothers thought could they encourage more people to buy cars—which would need their tires one day—if they began publishing a guide to attractions, hotels and restaurants throughout the country. The Michelin Guide positioned the company as more than just a tire brand and set it on a course to be recognized as an international cultural curator.

For centuries, the one who provides the market with the best stories, entertainment and information has been the one who will slaughter those who just want to sell products or services.

Ben Franklin, John Deere, Michelin and Casey Neistat demonstrate how any business leader can adopt a similar approach. Once YouTube, Facebook, LinkedIn and other platforms firmly established themselves as brand-building fixtures, producing consistent, original online content became the new baseline. In other words, regardless of your industry, if you are not producing relevant, audience-focused content, you don't exist.

In the 21st century, you are no longer a media buyer. The future belongs to media *creators*. Few understand this new reality better than an Austrian-based company that sold their first energy drink on April 1, 1987. As of 2020, Red Bull owned about 25% of the U.S. market while selling more than 7 billion cans globally. Over five decades, Red Bull built its reputation through hosting and sponsoring extreme sports events, beginning in 1988 with the ultimate in team relay races, the Dolomitenmann. An intimidating, exhilarating event that has birthed a thousand hardcore legends, it combines four merciless disciplines: mountain running, paragliding, whitewater kayaking and mountain biking. Other extreme events followed, such as Crashed Ice and Flugtag, and Red Bull has kept extending the brand to include pro soccer and hockey, Formula 1, NASCAR, music festivals and more.

It's never crowded along the extra mile and, on May 22, 2005, Red Bull boldly ventured into an arena few other brands dared to enter.

In their first season with Aston Martin, they launched a novel idea at the Monaco Grand Prix F1 race. Prior to the event, a Red Bull editorial team assembled stories, features, FAQs and photos about the drivers. The bulk of the magazine was laid out and ready to go before race time. They also hauled a one-ton printing press to the track. As soon as the checkered flag was waving at the finish line, a glossy publication with the final race results and standings was ready to be handed to fans leaving the venue.

It was a pivotal moment in which an energy drink brand made a strategic decision to create its own media company.

That decision has since morphed into Red Bull Media House, a global media company that spans 170 countries and 36 languages, with original content available across multiple TV, mobile, digital, audio and print platforms. Nobody back then could have imagined how the *Red Bulletin* magazine would evolve into a separate media entity, complete with television programming, documentaries, music studio, merchandising and a YouTube channel with more than 10 million subscribers and almost 6,000 videos. Red Bull's long-term brand strategy is a classic example of disruptive thinking straight out of *Moneyball*, the writings of Marshall McLuhan or Casey Neistat's videos: make everything revolve around a single, powerful concept and create online content that has the potential to attract an audience—even if those people don't care about energy drinks.

Red Bull's killer combination of their initial, low-cost guerilla marketing events followed by a long-term strategy focused on storytelling and event sponsorship was revolutionary in the marketing world. Essentially, Red Bull became a media company that happens to sell an energy drink, not the other way around.

You don't need to be a massive global conglomerate like Red Bull to succeed with this approach. The size of your enterprise doesn't matter. Whether you are an artisan, architect, attorney, repair shop, realtor, window manufacturer or struggling minor-league baseball team, you can deploy the same strategy and create your own Mona Lisa Effect.

Digital Fluency with Fresh "A-Peel"!

When they launched the expansion the Savannah Bananas in 2016, Jesse and Emily Cole had no marketing budget to speak of. As Jesse explains, "You don't need a marketing plan, you need an attention plan. Attention beats marketing 1000% of the time. We post videos every single week of our people. We've had millions of video views on Facebook, Twitter, Instagram and YouTube. From Opening Day in 2016, we made a commitment to use video to showcase who the people were behind the Bananas."

The Savannah Bananas are no different from any small-to medium-sized business who makes a choice to see things differently. Jesse will be the first to tell you that he's "in the entertainment business, where a baseball game happens to break out from time to time." The self-created attention his team generates attracts eyeballs 365 days a year thanks to a highly active YouTube channel with ongoing programs like *Behind the Bunch* and the behind-the-scenes *Bananas Unpeeled*. The way Jesse sees it, "People buy from the people behind the brand, not just the brand."

The next wave for the Bananas' web-based attention strategy is focused on creating even more personalized content for their growing fan base. Not even the global pandemic of 2020 could keep the Bananas down. After re-opening the ballpark with social distancing protocols in place, the Bananas made their own headfirst slide into the world of livestreaming. Games were viewed live by hardcore fans from Queens, Quebec, Qatar and everywhere in between. Jesse and his team of videographers are re-imagining the baseball viewing experience with drones, multiple camera viewpoints and live microphones on players and coaches. Using interactive platforms, fans can also play a role by voting and offering input on everything from player uniforms to the walk-up music for a hitter.

With shoestring budgets and no formal training, Casey Neistat and the Savannah Bananas parallel a similar success pattern to that experienced by the hyperactive son of immigrants from Belarus.

Gary was just three years old when his family left home in search of a better life in America. Soon, he was hustling through his childhood, running lemonade stands and selling baseball cards. As a kid, he fell in love with the New York Jets. By 2006—a year after YouTube went live—Gary launched a daily video show called *Wine Library TV*. His sharply pointed wine critiques and celebrity guests such as James Cramer, Wayne Gretzky and Dick Vermeil helped grow his parents' New Jersey–based wine business from $2 million annually to a $60 million e-commerce juggernaut.

After a thousand episodes of *Wine Library TV*, Gary "Vee" Vaynerchuk expanded his digital footprint with a massively successful YouTube channel, Facebook page and podcast with huge followings on Twitter and Instagram. Along the way he founded VaynerMedia, a digital marketing agency with a client roster featuring Fortune 100 companies like Pepsi, GE and Anheuser-Busch. A five-time *New York Times*-bestselling author, Gary Vee was crystal clear when he appeared with Seth Godin and other thought leaders on a Toronto stage in September 2016 at the first-ever Archangel Summit.

"You are a media company first. You are a _____ company second."

Apple, Nike and Red Bull are media companies that happen to sell phones, shoes and energy drinks. Dollar Shave Club, the Gold & Silver, the Savannah Bananas and Canada's Huggable Car Dealer are media companies that happen to sell razor blades, second-hand items, baseball tickets and used cars.

It's taken about 300 years for content marketing to evolve from mechanical printing presses to digital platforms that spread stories at the speed of light. Anyone from anywhere can make a decision to pick up their mobile device and participate. Or not. Participation does not come, however, without its hurdles, challenges and social obligations.

Lifestyle commentator Jenna Marbles became a social media rock star after uploading a 2010 video entitled "How to Trick People into Thinking You're Good Looking." Amassing an audience of 20 million subscribers, Jenna's quirky, edgy content explores fashion and beauty trends, social gaffes, personal faux pas and life with four dogs. She became the first social media star to have a wax figure displayed in Madame Tussauds Museum in New York City. On June 25, 2020, however, Jenna pulled her own plug and left YouTube in the wake of backlash from several videos posted in 2011 and 2012.

Born and raised in Rochester, New York, Jenna Marbles (real name Jenna Nicole Mourey) came clean in a tearful, emotional apology for having produced videos depicting her wearing blackface, mocking Asians with rapping lyrics and being critical of women who, as she said it, "slept around." Claiming it was never her intent to hurt anyone or make anyone feel ashamed, she announced her decision to switch offensive old content to "private."

The Jenna Marbles story is a cautionary tale. It reminds any content creator of the fine line between what is considered good taste (and in the public interest) and how those standards coexist on permanent social media platforms when subjected to changing societal standards. For close to a decade the Jenna Marbles brand was a YouTube powerhouse. One of the top female creators, she ran a channel that was once ranked as the 16th most followed in the world. Carelessness on social media can create disastrous consequences.

Despite these challenges, many top global brands are committed to following this new media playbook, including Red Bull, Nike, Ferrari, Patagonia and many others. Big Little Legends like the Savannah Bananas also demonstrate how to get your brand noticed in a noisy world. From day one, Jesse and Emily Cole applied their own *Moneyball* mindset to the promotion of their Coastal Plain League franchise without depending on enormous injections of cash or being held hostage by media gatekeepers and conglomerates. As of December 2020, the Bananas ranked #1 on TikTok with more followers (325,000) and more likes (5.6 million) than every team in Major League Baseball combined. It would have been damn near impossible for any 20th-century small business to attract more eyeballs than the equivalent to the New York Yankees, L.A. Dodgers or Chicago Cubs in a respective category.

Any leader can promote a culture of video storytelling and produce high-quality content within their organization.

Any company, large or small, from any industry or sector, can be in complete control of both message and medium.

Timeless Takeaways

#1. Be your own media company.

Nothing is holding you back. Nothing is stopping you from doing exactly what Casey Neistat, Gary Vee, Red Bull, Nike, Jack Daniel's, Dollar Shave Club, Canada's Huggable Car Dealer, the Savannah Bananas and thousands of others are doing with their brands.

With an appreciative nod to Marshall McLuhan, it's easy to see that while 20th-century marketing dinosaurs once roamed the earth and interrupted rented audiences with their commercials, the 21st century affords anyone the opportunity to build, grow and own a community as you see fit. Never before have brands and consumers had the ability to create and consume content at scale, communicate in real time with each other and do so without breaking the bank. Creating and publishing original content is now the cost of entry for building an irresistible brand. It's the gateway to long-term relationships and the difference between building a brand or being in sales.

#2. Think and act like a reporter.

How will your brand attract positive attention every day? What makes you truly different? What stories could you share that real people will actually care about? To adopt a reporter's mindset is to continually ask: "Why would anyone really give a s**t?"

Content is not an ad that reeks of being self-serving, "spammy" or salesy. To qualify, content must be any or all of four things: a) entertaining, b) educational, c) informative or d) inspiring. Two guys at a roofing company debating an upcoming Red Sox–Yankees series on Facebook will never be mistaken for professional sportscasters. But that post could potentially appeal to diehard baseball fans who might give those roofers a call one day when they need those services. Baseball trash talk humanizes their brand with culturally relevant, potentially informative or entertaining content that cements connection and trust. Clever, witty, good-natured exchanges about the Green Monster or the House That Ruth Built is radically different content from running "Ricky the Roofer" ads announcing 40% off shingle repairs—this month only.

Before going halfway around the world on Nike's nickel and uploading his high-flying adventures on April 9, 2012, Casey Neistat was going viral with videos that cost $40 to produce.

Later that same year, on October 14, 2012, Red Bull sponsored a world-record skydiving event where Austrian Felix Baumgartner parachuted to earth from nearly 25 miles into the stratosphere at Mach 1.25. In both cases—regardless of budget—these are stories that attract interest and fascinate people from different backgrounds, countries and demographics. What could you report on that would surprise your audience? Can you share stuff they don't already know?

#3. Marketing is no longer something you *buy*.
Today, marketing is something you need to *be*.

Are you ready to let the audience see the real you, beyond products or services you represent? This strategy is less about hacking algorithms, relying on SEO or re-targeting consumers who visit your website. Leaders need to recognize the new role they play in re-focusing their marketing efforts by asking, "What value does this content bring to the consumer first, rather than the business?"

Since the global pandemic of 2020, the death of George Floyd, massive public unrest and mob-like events that marked the end of Donald Trump's presidency, modern consumers are as politically and socially conscious as ever. It's not easy to build trust in an age of confrontation. You have more sensitivities and constituencies to consider than ever before. However, you can't be a leader and not put your best foot forward in the digital space. To be a great leader and build an irresistible brand begins and ends with being an ethical person who uses relevant technology to share stories and represent something more than utilitarian products and services.

Recapping Today's Headlines

Building a successful media company is *not* about the viral hit. It's not searching for simple hacks or trying to game an ungameable system. It is, however, about being a consistent contributor. It demands a mindset similar to what makes *Moneyball* much more than a baseball story. Billy Beane's quest for truth depicts the courage to ask disruptive, pointed questions no one else dares to ask. Metaphorically, *Moneyball* shines a glaring light on the future of modern marketing.

What if we need to stop asking short-term, self-serving questions like, "Why aren't we generating revenue with our marketing efforts?" What if, rather, leaders need to be asking this: "Are we creating delight with the content we deliver?" *Moneyball* revealed how an entire business and brand strategy can turn on a single question. Once a leader like Billy Beane began asking entirely new questions, he developed sharper focus. He started doing what well-heeled competitors were not. While the Yankees, Red Sox and Dodgers focused on opening coffers to purchase *star players*, the cash-strapped Oakland A's focused on sticking to a budget and buying *runs and wins*.

Like Wayne Gretzky, Billy Beane and *Moneyball*, authors Joe Pulizzi and Robert Rose skated way ahead of their time with the 2017 release of *Killing Marketing*. Together, they advanced the revolutionary idea of companies transforming marketing from being an expense to a profit center. Pointing to Red Bull as an example, Rose explains, "Since media has been democratized, consumers no longer need the media in order to make choices or discuss which brands they do business with. This means if I am a CEO, I know consumers will seek out and find information, entertainment and inspiration about products and services our firm offers. It can be us, or it can be our competitors. If I manage a business—I want it to be us."

For leaders and marketers, it's simple: business as usual *isn't*. Either you become your own media company and build awareness and reputational equity or allow competitors to beat you to the punch. Acting and thinking like a media company is the only strategic option still available in today's attention economy.

This is not a one-off campaign. This is a decades-long commitment.

Becoming a media company is how you enter the ballpark and put your brand in a position to swing for the fences.

How will you make it count?

*We shape our tools and
thereafter our tools shape us.*

MARSHALL MCLUHAN

PART IV

BIGGER
THAN YOUR
BACKYARD

10

SPARKLE LIKE WORLDCHANGERS

Discover the Beauty of Higher Purpose

February 2, 2014

Suppose you lived in a remote location without substantial means or powerful connections. How would you go about the serious business of changing the world if you constantly felt economically, culturally and socially subjugated in every way?

Would your sparkle shine through as you surmounted daily barriers that include ethnicity, established dogma, gender and geography? Could you forsake the comforts of emotional safety and social approval in exchange for a life of service and adventure? Or would you fold like a lawn chair when faced with rejection and criticism?

For those who choose this path, history offers its share of examples to follow, including a formidable Black woman from the Deep South, orphaned at age seven. She then lived with her sister, but was treated so cruelly by her sister's husband that she left that home to marry by age 14. Much later, this vocal woman became an influential, self-made millionaire who shared her ideas on entrepreneurial skills and social reform with anyone willing to listen.

She acquired upscale properties in Indianapolis and Chicago, as well as a magnificent, 30-room Italian Renaissance mansion dubbed Villa Lewaro by her friend, legendary opera singer Enrico Caruso. A stylish woman of wealth and taste—and sympathy—she encouraged others to better their lives. In her words, "Don't sit and wait for opportunities. You have to get up and make them. If I have accomplished any-thing in life, it is because I have been willing to work hard."

If you're thinking this independent, strong-willed female tycoon was destined for TV stardom, you would be mis-taken. Television wasn't invented back then. In fact, Sarah Breedlove passed away about six months after the final shot was fired in World War I. One of six children, Sarah grew up in an impoverished Louisiana village, with no formal educa-tion to speak of. Widowed with a two-year-old daughter by age 19, Sarah started with $2 and a dream before becoming America's first self-made female millionaire. According to the Guinness World Records, she is the first woman in his-tory to have started with nothing and gone on to amass a million-dollar fortune.

She hobnobbed with glitterati that included presidential advisors and established a philanthropic legacy that contin-ues to this day. If Sarah were still alive, her TED Talk would be viewed and shared by millions curious to know how anyone could prosper in the face of so many obstructions. Nearly a century before Oprah Winfrey entered our collec-tive living rooms, Sarah was inspiring leaders at a time when lynching was commonplace and women were still battling for the right to vote in free elections.

And then there is Rachel, born in a different country and a later era. Starting from her kitchen table, Rachel made jewelry just for the sheer fun of it. Entranced by the elegance of favorite aunts Ginnie and Louise, six-year-old Rachel was bitten hard by the fashion bug while rummaging through their closets and devouring *Vogue* magazines. Growing up in football-crazy and hockey-mad Saskatchewan, she was forced to be a tomboy thanks to two older brothers. But Rachel dreamed of a much different world, one that offered a stylish alternative to her humble surroundings in Regina's sleepy north end. Fashion capitals of the world like Paris, Milan and New York were worlds away—a distant, far-fetched fantasy.

Across the country in rural Nova Scotia, a woman named Barb set out on a mission to improve lives and initiate social change through commerce. Raised by a single mother who depended on welfare benefits, she has vivid memories of watching people drop off Christmas hampers and drive away from their trailer. She recalled, "My sister and I didn't want handouts. We wanted to be invited to the banquet." Barb had no way of knowing how many banquets would later be held in her honor.

Sarah Breedlove might have recognized kindred spirits and business soul sisters in Rachel Mielke and Barb Stegemann. What began with Rachel tinkering with clippers, pliers and gemstones at her kitchen table evolved into a jewelry juggernaut with a team of nearly 150, a thriving web-based business, national wholesale partnerships and ten corporately owned stores. Her Hillberg & Berk products have been worn at the 2008 Academy Awards and the 2016 Rio Olympics, and two of her original pieces are part of a private collection owned by Her Majesty Queen Elizabeth II. Meanwhile, Barb disrupted the traditional perfume industry with a collection of fragrances called the 7 Virtues. Launching her brand in 2012, Barb created a line of exotic scents that sources essential oils from war-torn Afghanistan. Her 7 Virtues line was the first Canadian brand featured in the Clean at Sephora program.

Through social entrepreneurship, this Halifax-based activist brings peace and prosperity to some of the world's hottest trouble spots. Her uplifting story has been shared by media the world over, including CNN, *Forbes*, *Fast Company*, *Cosmopolitan* and *Vogue*.

Sarah, Barb and Rachel are three women who overcame hardscrabble backgrounds to create unlimited opportunity for others. Each battled against various degrees of sexism, prejudice, hate, greed, jealousy and cruelty every bloody step of the way. I think Sarah, Barb and Rachel would all nod their heads and confirm that the battle for dignity demands a steep price. Only through bedrock principles such as courage, self-respect and personal accountability did they demonstrate what it takes to create self-sustaining communities.

Any journey of a thousand miles is always activated by a first, uncertain step. Ideally, that step begins with a deeply personal connection to a cause much bigger than oneself. An idea and vision that reaches in and grabs your soul by the throat. Refuses to let go. It's how three different women from different countries wound up changing the world, including their own.

With a triple bottom line impact.

Sustaining People, Profit and the Planet

Introduced in 1994, "triple bottom line" is a sustainability framework that indicates a company's economic, environmental and social impact. Coined by British sustainability guru John Elkington, triple bottom line is a way to measure and manage corporate performance to achieve financial return while improving lives and protecting Mother Earth. An avid cyclist and author of 20 books, Elkington contends that if a firm only looks at profitability while ignoring people and planet, it cannot render a full account of the real cost of doing business. Sadly, like many genius-level concepts that arrived far before their time, Elkington's TBL morphed into a business buzzword, too often reduced to a form of accounting propaganda.

Once his original theory was diluted by armies of corporate bean counters, TBL became just another set of KPIs—key performance indicators—gathered by organizations desperate to give themselves a numerically validated pat on the back. According to Elkington, TBL was intended to be a new genetic code, a practical tool to provoke leaders into deeper thinking about the future of capitalism.

Back in the 1800s, lofty ideas from global management consultants were the furthest thing from Sarah Breedlove's mind when she departed the Mississippi Delta and headed north to St. Louis. Still in her early 20s, she started suffering from hair loss through a scalp ailment called alopecia. She worked long hours as a cook and washerwoman, and after a few years her second marriage collapsed. Struggling as a sole provider, she later told the *New York Times* that life at 35 was anything but certain and stable. "As I bent over the wash-board and looked at my arms buried in soapsuds, I said to myself: 'What are you going to do when you grow old and your back gets stiff? Who is going to take care of your little girl?'"

With necessity as her divine mother of invention, Sarah began experimenting with hair treatments and creams while learning the inner workings of the beauty industry. Starting with seed capital of $1.25, she developed her own original theories and secret recipes for reversing hair loss. Sarah believed her homemade batches of hair remedies could help other women of color who weren't getting what they needed from products being sold by white cosmetic firms designed for white women. Promoting the idea that her treatments were geared to the unique needs of Black women, Sarah created hair growing tonics, strengtheners, hot combs, and facial treatments. She began chatting up her creations with friends at church groups and started selling products door to door. Word about her mixtures and potions spread like wildfire, and Sarah realized she had landed on a persuasive idea that spoke a truth that other folks cared deeply about.

By 1905, Sarah, her daughter and her maturing business relocated to Denver, where she re-married, re-named and re-branded herself as "Madam C.J. Walker." She started hiring and training other women to be Walker Agents, pro-moting her philosophy of "cleanliness and loveliness" to advance the status of African American women.

She scaled the business with a huge mail order depart-ment and opened a beauty school in Pittsburgh that taught the Walker Method of hair growing. In 1910, she relocated to Indianapolis, built a new factory and expanded the

Walker System into a national network of 40,000 licensed sales agents earning healthy commissions across the U.S., Central America and the Caribbean.

Long before television and the internet, Madam C.J. Walker (formerly known as Sarah Breedlove) discovered it was possible to synthesize profit, purpose and beauty through a compelling idea bigger than herself. To nurture and inspire her growing community, she hosted her company's first annual conference in Philadelphia in the summer of 1917 with about 200 delegates—an event believed to be one of the first-ever national gatherings for female entrepreneurs. Walker awarded prizes to women with top sales and significant charitable contributions. Long before John Elkington shared his theoretical views on triple bottom line, Madam C.J. Walker was showing how anyone could make an honest buck—without exploitation.

Before her passing in 1919, Walker had become a generous donor to the NAACP's anti-lynching campaign, had bankrolled college scholarships for Black students and had assisted countless Black artists and musicians. Addressing the annual convention of the National Negro Business League, she declared, "I am a woman who came from the cotton fields of the South. From there I was promoted to the washtub. From there, I was promoted to cook. And from there, I promoted myself into the business of manufacturing hair goods and built my own factory on my own ground. Everybody told me I was making a mistake." In 1998, the U.S. Postal Service issued a commemorative stamp in her honor. In 2016, Sundial Brands launched a new collection of hair-care products inspired by Madam Walker's legacy.

And in 2020, Netflix released *Self Made: Inspired by the Life of Madam C.J. Walker*, a dramatic series based on the biography *On Her Own Ground*, written by Walker's great-great granddaughter, A'Lelia Bundles.

If you're prepared to answer a similar calling, be prepared to encounter a multitude of people who think you're making a big mistake. Critics go with this territory. Always have. Bricks and bouquets comprise the predictable pattern for any entrepreneurial revolution—like the one launched in 1963 by a woman from Harris County, Texas, fed up the wazoo with being passed over for promotions and pay raises so less qualified men could climb the company ladder. With a life savings of $5,000, Mary Kay Ash launched her own beauty line, opening a tiny storefront in Dallas. It was the first bold step toward inspiring hundreds of thousands of other women to achieve personal and financial success— and their own shiny pink Cadillac. Or take Coco Chanel. The daughter of a street peddler, Chanel was 12 when her mother died and she was shipped off to an orphanage. Founder of The Body Shop, Anita Roddick, was the daughter of immigrants, born in a bomb shelter in Littlehampton, England. Oprah Winfrey was the daughter of an unwed teen mom in Kosciusko, Mississippi, and spent much of her rural childhood wearing potato sacks as dresses.

Many other courageous leaders have refused to settle for crumbs, play small or follow conventional routes. In her early 20s, Sara Blakely worked at Disney and sold fax machines before being rejected numerous times by potential investors in the garment industry. The founder of Spanx became the world's youngest self-made female billionaire and never took a nickel of outside investment to grow or scale—an unheard-of feat in such enterprises. Don't be shocked or surprised when everyone doesn't immediately see incredible merit in your new, visionary idea. You just need a few committed core believers who already know that accepted rules can be silly and absurd. You need to surround yourself with the kind of people who also want to shake things up and give status quo a swift kick in the behind.

Changing the World Starts at the Edge

As Madam C.J. Walker proved, alignment of purpose, profit and protecting the planet hinges on attracting people who already share similar values. In the beginning, her earliest converts were fellow seekers: cash-strapped women willing to jump in with both feet—and bring their friends. Real change, the stuff of which legends are made, only happens on the fringes. Outside of commercial, cultural, political or social mainstreams. It doesn't necessarily require access to capital or influential people. It can begin with who you want to help, and how far you'll go to help them. That's precisely how it happened with Rachel Mielke and Barb Stegemann.

After making her first-ever necklace with freshwater pearls, Swarovski crystals and Bali sterling silver, Rachel thought, "This makes me feel special. I want to find a way to share this feeling with other women." In April 2005, while working at a Regina non-profit, she was convinced by a close friend to take her hobby and put it behind a booth at a three-day nursing convention. In utter disbelief, Rachel watched customers clamor to purchase her handcrafted earrings, bracelets and necklaces. She sold out her entire inventory. Every last shiny, shimmering, glittering piece. Exclaiming "wow, wow, just wow!" many times over, Rachel was shaking her head throughout the whole event.

Repeatedly, she counted the cash in her hand. Her initial $500 investment had miraculously turned into $5,000. It was the "a-ha!" moment when Rachel realized that making jewelry was her true passion. She had tangible evidence of how market demand collided with her own personal inspiration in a wonderfully profitable way. After two years of working the business part-time, she ventured out on her own, re-branding the company as Hillberg & Berk to honor great-grandmother Hilda Bergman and her dog, a miniature pinscher named Berkeley.

Launching a luxury jewelry business in the heart of the Canadian prairies is not for the faint of heart. There are not as many high-end shoppers in Regina, Saskatchewan, as you would see on New York's Fifth Avenue or Rodeo Drive in L.A. Bone-chilling, brutally cold winter months force potential customers to stay inside their cozy warm homes, so Rachel's business demanded plenty of patience and enormous sacrifice, such as dipping into her own salary to pay her first employee. For many months she rode the razor's edge, keeping the company afloat on maxed-out credit. Never once did she waver in her conviction. Rachel knew what happened at the initial trade show was real: there was demand for her products and people were willing to pay top dollar. So, the only daughter of a blue-collar electrician hung in there. More importantly, she kept pitching in to help local non-profit organizations with different fundraisers, donating time, expertise and jewelry to help those in need.

Around the same time that Rachel was battling to get her company financially healthy, Barb was in Nova Scotia putting the finishing touches on her first book.

Drawing from the enduring wisdom of great philosophers like Socrates, Plato and Marcus Aurelius, *The 7 Virtues of a Philosopher Queen* is a practical guide for any woman looking to live, lead and make a difference in an illogical world. Barb describes her book as a set of guiding principles leaders have used for centuries to navigate through chaotic, difficult times of war and conflict. Like the time her best friend almost died after his head was nearly split in two with a crushing blow from a Taliban ax on March 4, 2006.

Trevor never saw it coming. No one did.

A Canadian Forces peacekeeper in Afghanistan, Captain Trevor Greene was speaking with village elders in Kandahar Province about bringing in clean water and health care. At a peaceful shura (a consultation ceremony that forbids weapons) Trevor respected tribal custom and, in a gesture of goodwill, laid down his rifle and removed his combat helmet. That's when a 16-year-old boy suddenly attacked from behind, shattering Captain Greene's skull. Preyed upon by terrorists, the boy had been offered $5 to kill a soldier.

Before the attacker could swing his weapon a second time, Trevor's comrades with the Seaforth Highlanders shot and killed him. Then they saw brain matter oozing from a hole in the back of Trevor's head. He received life-saving emergency treatment on a U.S. Army medivac helicopter before undergoing surgery at a Canadian hospital at Kandahar Air Field.

Once stabilized, Trevor was airlifted to a military hospital in Germany before being sent back home to convalesce at Vancouver General Hospital, where he spent weeks in a coma.

Doctors advised his fiancée, Debbie, to move on with her life.

After undergoing two bilateral cranioplasties, Trevor began many years of physiotherapy and speech therapy. Keeping him company on that long road to recovery was his friend Barb from their King's College days in Halifax. The two had met while studying sociology and journalism and forged a tight platonic friendship—one that was now being put to the ultimate test. Barb vividly recalls how Trevor would persist for hours to press a single BlackBerry key. With no clue how she was going to do it, Barb vowed to carry on with his Afghanistan mission and make it her own.

She became hell-bent on doing her part to bring peace to the region. Like Madam C.J. Walker, she refused to believe that she was powerless to change things. She stepped into a new kind of power.

Buying power. Specifically, the buying power of women.

When Character Becomes Your Destiny

For Rachel, her destiny shifted when the phone rang in the fall of 2013 at her downtown Regina office. On the line was the private secretary of Saskatchewan's lieutenant-governor, Vaughn Solomon Schofield. In hushed tones, she informed Rachel she had a highly confidential matter to discuss.

It would be best if they met in person.

A few days later, Schofield's private secretary walked into Rachel's office, closed the door and said, "We don't have much of a budget, but we're eager to know if you'll take this project on." With her brain exploding like flashbulbs, Rachel immediately recalled crossing paths with Schofield at a number of charity events to support causes such as cancer care, Habitat for Humanity and the YWCA. Dumbfounded, she listened and learned how the lieutenant-governor had been granted an audience at Buckingham Palace with Her Majesty Queen Elizabeth II and wanted to present a gift on behalf of her loyal subjects in Saskatchewan.

Pinching herself many times over, Rachel kicked into conceptual mode, knowing she had just invested heavily in some rare cut gems that might be appropriate for one of history's longest reigning monarchs. She couldn't really afford that recent $10,000 shipment of Madagascar tourmaline stones, but Rachel felt they were just too beautiful to send back. They would be perfect for a one-of-kind creation for the sovereign: a flower-based brooch representing both strength and softness. Strikingly modern, the white gold, diamond-encrusted purple tourmaline brooch was quite unlike anything the Queen had in her extensive, carefully selected royal collection.

Rachel was on pins and needles. "I remember feeling extremely excited, but also quite unsure. I had no idea whether she would like it, let alone wear it," she said. Four months after the $15,000 gift was presented to Her Majesty, the phone rang once again at Rachel's office.

February 2, 2014, was the day one world became another.

> Hey Rachel... CBC is on the line and they want your
> reaction to the Queen wearing your brooch to church in
> Sandringham.

Immediately, Rachel flipped open her laptop and stared in
disbelief at the Google images she was seeing. Staring back
at her were photos of the most powerful woman in the world
wearing her creation. The story was trending on Twitter. It
was making a big splash in the *Daily Mail* and other British
newspapers.

Everybody in Rachel's office stopped what they were
doing. They started screaming, crying and high-fiving while
doing one of the biggest happy dances in provincial history.
Within the week, Rachel was interviewed by upward of
20 media outlets, including national TV coverage that catapulted Hillberg & Berk onto the world stage. Overnight,
Rachel Mielke had suddenly joined the international elite
of jewelry designers from her single-store operation in
Saskatchewan.

Fueled by this royalty-inspired reputation for prairie
glamor, Rachel's small company quickly grew tenfold, going
from about $1 million in annual sales to more than $10 million. What was once a one-woman, kitchen-table business
now serves customers in more than 40 countries and has
contributed to countless charitable causes. Celebrities like
Carrie Underwood, Sarah McLachlan, Michelle Obama,
Barbara Walters and Celine Dion are just a few owners of her
handcrafted designs. In the meantime, Queen Elizabeth II
added yet another rarefied Hillberg & Berk piece to her collection. Presented by Governor-General David Johnston to

commemorate the Queen's 65th anniversary and Canada's 150th birthday, the exquisite Sapphire Jubilee brooch took eight months to complete and features more than 400 diamonds and 48 Canadian sapphires—from the only known Canadian deposits of the gem, located on Nunavut's Baffin Island. Calling her the original empowered woman, Rachel says Her Majesty is "a symbol of strength and inspiration for all women and people around the world; one who truly defines what sparkle means to us."

Since its inception in 2007, Hillberg & Berk has been on a mission to be a company that empowers women "one sparkle at a time." They have donated well over $2 million in cash and $8 million in products to a variety of charitable organizations that provide opportunities to women all over Canada and globally. Each International Women's Day, Hillberg & Berk creates a special piece, like the Venus pin, in support of women's issues, with 100% of proceeds aimed at ending human trafficking in Canada. Besides supporting multiple hospital foundations, Rachel has also funded several university scholarships for women and supported the establishment of a collective of jewelry makers in Myanmar, promoting peace through inter-faith job creation. Her company personifies the spirit of John Elkington's triple bottom line, integrating philanthropy with profitability while running a business and brand that cares deeply about the people it serves.

More than 3,000 miles to the east, Barb Stegemann surfed the web and discovered two crucial pieces of information about Afghanistan. The first was a story about an essential-oils distiller named Abdullah Arsala trying to support his tribe by creating legal crops of orange blossom instead of adding to the poppy crops that account for 90% of the world's heroin supply. Next, Barb learned that if Afghan farmers were paid fairly for their essential oils, they would have the cash and confidence to refuse to grow Taliban opium. Maybe she could prevent some other kid from being hired to kill for $5.

With no financial backing or expertise on how to make perfume, Barb called Abdullah and bought $2,000 worth of orange-blossom oil on her Visa. Little did she know how much that fateful decision would wield a different kind of power in the fight against war, poverty, drugs and patriarchal terrorism. One credit card purchase would trigger a domino effect and reduce Taliban influence while creating jobs for others. It wasn't the most conventional way to start a business, but, like any self-starter, Barb wasn't restricted by convention. Maybe it had to do with growing up in an economically deprived area near Antigonish, Nova Scotia. Maybe it was the way she put herself through university and raised two children as a single mom. Or, maybe her friend Trevor's horrific accident was the catalyst that led her to step off that cliff in May of 2010 and make her most daunting decision of all.

Armed with a homemade business plan and two months of home-grown sales, Barb walked boldly onto a soundstage on the 10th floor of the CBC building in Toronto to pitch her idea in the *Dragons' Den*.

It was an all-or-nothing gamble to see if a panel of Canada's most hard-nosed, jaded business elites would provide the much-needed financial backing for her project. She confidently proposed an idea for a different kind of perfume company. After hearing the tragic story that inspired her mission, two of the Dragons fought back tears. Three wanted to invest. The Mona Lisa Effect was about to be unleashed.

Within a year, Barb's 7 Virtues perfume line was on display in Hudson's Bay stores across Canada, generating $500,000 in sales and disrupting the status quo in a $29 billion global industry. With "Make Perfume, Not War" as a Tribal Narrative, Barb's company sources oils from farmers in Afghanistan, Haiti, Rwanda and the Middle East. A self-described "retail activist," she explains her revolutionary business model this way:

> As a woman in this patriarchy, I didn't have a way to touch peace. I am not a brave soldier or world leader. But I realized women own buying power; we own voting power. So, I created a new way. I wrote a book to empower women to harness our buying and voting power to reverse cycles of war and poverty. It's more than building a business for profit. It's building a business with purpose.

Barb's business model ensures that everyone in the supply chain—farmer, supplier, retailer and her company—is fairly compensated while the 7 Virtues brand message continues to spread. Based on her 2008 bestseller, she also launched a network of book clubs for women who share similar values, with 7 Virtues fragrances offered to attendees. Barb is now an in-demand speaker throughout North America, and always leaves a lasting impression with her audiences. In her words, "No one can teach you how to become yourself.

Some people are fortunate to find a clear path in their youth. Others recreate themselves mid-life."

More than 7 billion people inhabit our planet, but many in first world nations prefer to cross their fingers, wait and hope for a "big break" or lottery win. Others hang out at local coffee shops, grousing, moaning and whining about how they would do things differently if only someone would give them a chance.

Regardless of our station in life, anyone can choose to be an agent of possibility. An orphaned daughter of enslaved parents in Louisiana, a self-made Saskatchewan fashionista and a single mom from rural Nova Scotia fought hard for social and economic justice while becoming champions for peace and prosperity through entrepreneurship. No one ever cast a ballot and elected Madam C.J. Walker, Rachel Mielke or Barb Stegemann to a position of power. None were handed huge marketing budgets on silver platters or had a ready-made audience of thousands eager to support and evangelize their cause. Self-starting Big Little Legends from different places and periods in history demonstrate that charisma and access to capital pales in comparison to being a leader fortified with a clearly defined mission and purpose propelled by the irresistible forces of Strategic Drama.

Timeless Takeaways

#1. Dream big. Start small.

A grand vision begins with rock-solid roots. The surest way to know if your game-changing idea has real merit is to test your disruptive concept on any small group of like-minded people. Can you find five to ten people who might be floored by your concept? Are you able to pass the "check writing" test? Unless real people reach into their pockets and hand over real money, your idea is essentially worthless.

No proven formula or step-by-step checklist offers a straight line to connect any leader to an idea that will inspire a community. The fan base for brands like *Pawn Stars*, Pike Place Fish Market, Casey Neistat, Chapel Dulcinea, Dollar Shave Club, Hillberg & Berk and 7 Virtues all started with a handful of people who believed in what they were doing. How will you make your first five to ten people believe? If you find it's a struggle to inspire five individuals, can you reasonably expect to inspire 5,000?

#2. Done is way better than perfect.

Madam C.J. Walker would agree with this statement. So would Rachel, Barb, Rick Harrison, Jim and Dawna Gilbert and Jesse Cole. Perfectionism is a very real problem that prevents many creative and intelligent people from achieving their full potential. The sinister dark cloak of meticulous perfectionism prevents us from getting work out the door. Once you accept that every act of creation is a draft, you'll find it easier to get it done and out the door.

Done is the locomotive that drives the freight train of momentum through the barrier of resistance. *The War of Art* author Steven Pressfield describes "the Resistance" as a repelling force that threatens to stop creative activity by any means necessary, including rationalization, distractions, self-doubt, self-sabotage and much more. "Done is better than perfect" is a phrase that can remind you to kick your own butt when needed. General George S. Patton said it best: "A good plan today is better than a perfect plan tomorrow."

#3. Do you occupy a position of influence, or are you becoming a person of influence?

Unlike the Queen of England, not everyone has leadership status or power conferred upon them. Don't be fooled into thinking influence is a top-down construct flowing from a position of absolute authority. Gandhi, Martin Luther King Jr. and Rosa Parks never saw things that way. Neither did Mary Kay Ash, Coco Chanel or Sara Blakely.

Having a "position," like CEO, vice-president or business owner, provides a certain amount of influence, security and authority. If that position gets taken away, however, influence, security and authority also disappear. Real power—not artificially superimposed—originates from being a person who creates their own security from within. Investing tens of thousands of lonely hours to sharpen skills and hone expertise. Knowing how to make your product and bring it to market in a way that creates a triple bottom line impact. If you invest just ten hours a week for a year honing a specialized skill, you will be 500 hours ahead of the person who dreams but does nothing. Access to knowledge is cheap and easy. The desire to implement, refine and excel is rare.

A Beautiful Mindset

It costs nothing to build character. You don't require financial help or high-powered connections to work hard, ask pointed questions, speak frankly or develop your mind. It's what Trevor Greene has been so working so bloody hard to do.

The day he got his skull smashed in during a Taliban ambush was the day Trevor's real mission began. Teaming with Dr. Ryan D'Arcy, a neuroscientist from Simon Fraser University in Vancouver, Trevor has worked extremely hard to "rethink what's possible" in pushing the limits of neuro-plasticity in his brain. There wasn't a dry eye in the house during Ryan and Trevor's TEDx Talk in February 2020 as they shared penetrating insights on how shattered pieces can be put back together. Since that horrific attack, "Canada's Iron Soldier" and his wife, Debbie, are helping us understand the brain's ability to repair and rewire itself as he learns to walk again with help from an exoskeleton. In July 2010, Trevor and Debbie stood at the altar and exchanged vows while daughter Grace carried the rings down the aisle. Later that year, a stranger donated $100,000, which they used to establish the Greene Family Education Initiative Fund to help young Afghan women become teachers. In 2016, Trevor and Debbie proved impossible is just a word in the dictionary when they welcomed new son Noah into the world.

Together, Trevor and Debbie published *March Forth*, a remarkable story of their shared struggles of healing and love told in two voices. Struggles about the emotional and psychological scars of war, battles with PTSD and the incredible pressure of caring for an incapacitated spouse while raising small children. Struggles like failed cranioplasty surgery, and that moment when a teary-eyed Trevor had to endure a hose being jammed down his throat while a distraught Debbie kept thinking, "Nobody can take more of this."

When the chips are really down, you will find a way. Once you clearly know your "why," you can always find a "how."

Trevor's next book, his seventh, is focused on creating social enterprises.

I got my start by giving myself a start.
It is often the best way. I believe in
push and we must push ourselves.

MADAM C.J. WALKER

11

PLAY A LONGER GAME

Infinite Immortality on a Frozen Field of Dreams

September 12, 2000

Here is a story of a company located in a small town somewhere in Middle America.

The organization enjoyed sporadic periods of success
followed by some very lean years. Back-to-back decades of
futility through the 1970s and '80s. By the '90s, the financial writing was on the wall. Economic storm clouds were
gathering. If someone didn't make some drastic decisions,
this company ran the very real risk of going broke. That
someone—the person who had to make those decisions—
happened to be a long-time employee named Bob.

Originally from Des Moines, Iowa, Bob joined this
Wisconsin-based company in 1973, then worked his way up
from paper-pusher to senior executive. He was hard working. Well liked.

On June 5, 1989, Bob was appointed president and given
the Herculean task of turning the company's sagging fortunes around in a highly competitive landscape. His market
opponents were massive: big-time players flush with cash
and headquartered in flashy, big-league cities like New York,

Chicago, San Francisco, Dallas and Miami. His competitors possessed enormous financial clout and could suck any talent pool dry. Bob started to recognize an inescapable truth: his small town was trapped in a big-city business.

In a town with a population of only 105,000, money alone would not solve Bob's problem. It was going to require something else altogether.

Dire circumstances demanded something that a frequently overlooked, underestimated community could believe in. Something to rally around and return a small-town company to its former glory. Bob had no idea how he was going to pull a miracle rabbit out of his green and gold hat, but he knew he had to put vision before money.

It would take a lot of convincing. Many in the community were highly skeptical about the company's chances. Bob went door to door in neighborhoods and table to table in restaurants, trying to get folks onside. Not everyone was sold on his last-ditch pitch. Some doors were shut in his face. But he refused to roll over and quit.

Bob Harlan rolled up his sleeves and worked harder to save the nearly bankrupt, financially ailing Green Bay Packers.

A working-class city, Green Bay, Wisconsin, is surrounded by rural farmland. The heart of North America's smallest community to host a professional sports franchise is legendary Lambeau Field. This is pro football's answer to iconic venues such as Fenway Park, Yankee Stadium or Madison Square Garden. Stroll on the turf at Lambeau on any ordinary weekday afternoon, and it's glaringly obvious this is no ordinary sports facility. Lambeau Field looms large in the middle of a quiet residential neighborhood, sitting across the street from post-war homes that were already there when the stadium was first built in 1957 for the bargain-basement price of $960,000.

On any given weekday, a dozen or more stadium tours are available for wide-eyed tourists eager to trade time and money to get a non-game-day taste of the Green Bay Packer experience. Each year, upward of 200,000 people take these tours, soaking up the rich history of a team founded by Curly Lambeau in 1919. Expert guides regale their audiences with Packer anecdotes from yesteryear. Visitors gain insider knowledge at minute levels of detail that might bore the rest of the world but leaves football fans spellbound. Visitors also learn the team chant, repeated forward and backward: *Go Pack Go!*

The daily stadium tour is just a small part of a business model that didn't exist before Bob Harlan was named team president in 1989. As the NFL's only community-owned franchise, the Packers have been a non-profit organization since August 18, 1923, when the original articles of incorporation were filed with the state of Wisconsin. By the mid-1990s, league economics were changing dramatically, leaving Bob and his seven-member executive committee searching for new answers. Free agency and skyrocketing player salaries were wreaking havoc with Packers finances. Two bankers on his board of directors warned Bob the team was in serious trouble. A financial apocalypse was looming. They needed to find ways to generate additional, home-grown revenues. Although the Packers were getting a healthy chunk from lucrative network television deals, those dollars were shared with other teams around the NFL—not enough to cover shortfalls. One economic forecast predicted the Packers would be insolvent by 2005.

Escalating hard costs and lack of new revenues were threatening the future viability of one of the NFL's oldest franchises. In pro football terminology, Bob Harlan needed to drop back in the pocket and throw his own "Hail Mary."

Like Bart Starr, Brett Favre, Aaron Rodgers and other Packer quarterbacks of yesteryear, Bob had to scramble and toss a last-second desperation pass to turn defeat into impossible victory. And the more Bob thought, pondered and prayed, the more he wondered if the key to the Packers' future might be buried in their legendary past.

A Green and Golden Moment

Out of all the team's rich and glorious history, it's what's known as the "Lombardi era" that has made the biggest mark on the Packers' legacy. In 1959, rookie coach Vince Lombardi arrived in Green Bay from New York after the team had posted a record of 1-10-1. A single victory against ten defeats and a draw. Lombardi immediately reversed a decade of losing with a respectable 7-and-5 season. By the 1960 season, the Packers played in the NFL championship game. Before he was through, Lombardi would lead his team to an unprecedented collection of five league titles over a seven-year period. Tiny Green Bay became known far and wide as "Titletown U.S.A."

The 1960s Packers produced more than a dozen pro football Hall-of-Famers and a plethora of magnificent memories, highlighted by 1967's legendary "Ice Bowl." In minus-48-degree weather, Green Bay engineered a late fourth-quarter comeback with a game-winning drive in impossible, horrifically cold conditions. With 16 seconds to go, the Packers rallied to beat the Dallas Cowboys and became the first NFL team to capture a third straight title. The Ice Bowl became pro football's historical equivalent to boxing's "Rumble in the Jungle" or hockey's "Miracle on Ice."

No single event in NFL history has been referenced more times by the league's myth-making machine than the Ice Bowl. From that day forward, Lambeau Field would be forever known as the "Frozen Tundra": a fabled gridiron where the greatest gladiators of them all overcame a worthy opponent and a wickedly mean Mother Nature on one of her worst Arctic chill days. Many players on both teams felt the pain of frostbite for years afterward.

Multiple legends were made that day. Eternally, frozen in time.

Following that triumph over Dallas, the Packers captured their second straight Super Bowl title and Lombardi stepped down as head coach. Starting with the appointment of long since forgotten Phil Bengtson, the Packer faithful watched a revolving door of head coaches come and go. More than two decades of on-field misery ensued. With each "rebuilding program" came another effort to step away from the shadow of Lombardi's legacy and create something new. Each successive regime wanted to put their own stamp on things and establish their own form of success. But between

1968 and 1991, the Packers only went to the playoffs twice. Lombardi's decade of distinction became a faded memory, mired under the stink of a quarter century of futility. Top free agents and draft choices were refusing to play in what was dubbed as the NFL's version of Siberia.

The endearing throwback franchise was on the verge of extinction.

The more Bob looked around, however, the more he recognized everyone in Packerland was missing the point. The more the team's community—hardcore fans, coaching staff, front office, executive team—focused on the on-field woes, the further away they got from grasping the essence of the Packers' business and brand.

Bob calls it his "Green and Golden Moment."

On the one hand, the team had an antiquated business model centered on selling game-day tickets, hot dogs, beer, popcorn and souvenirs at a mere ten events each year. Two pre-season games and eight regular-season games represented the full extent of the Packers' ability to produce locally generated revenues—monies they didn't have to share with other NFL clubs. But on the other hand, Green Bay also possessed a rich championship history, celebrated and treasured nationwide thanks to the larger-than-life mythology and folklore created by NFL Films. Intangible assets from the league's highly respected propaganda machine were being ignored and overlooked.

Bob Harlan began pondering some entirely new questions.

What if the Packers stopped running away from their storied past? What if they decided instead to embrace that history and build on it?

Harlan knew that his idea might be the most defining moment in franchise history—aside from the 1959 hiring of Vince Lombardi. The stakes were high. If he failed to get people to buy into his long-term vision, the Packers might have to be sold, relocated to another city or cease operating.

The more Bob mulled it over, the more he knew they had to go big or go home. Instead of ten games a year, he envisioned a year-round cash cow that would produce revenues from retail stores, restaurants and meeting room rentals. To make this vision a reality, Bob needed Brown County voters to pony up for part of the $295 million price tag for renovating historic Lambeau Field. The proposal would forever alter the team's entire business model.

Bob unveiled his master plan in January 2000, not realizing he would be swept up into a contentious campaign. He took to the streets and stood outside many a Walmart. For every ten people he talked to, five adamantly opposed the idea. The community was split. Many citizens resisted the 0.5% sales tax required to execute Bob's plan. Folks just didn't want to pay any new tax. Going in, Bob had no inkling how difficult it would be to secure approval for the project.

By the time of the Brown County referendum to levy the tax, the battle had taken its toll. Bob was being roundly criticized in the media. His doctors warned the stress was affecting his health. Friends worried he might be on the verge of a heart attack. But he never gave up on his vision of restoration or his unwavering faith in the fans.

Following an uncertain nine months, judgment day arrived on September 12, 2000. Much to Bob's relief, the referendum passed—with 53% of the vote.

The final hurdle had been cleared. The little town that could stepped up and saved one of the most storied franchises in all of sports.

Turning Lambeau Field into a professional sports cathedral took three years. In the first season following the re-launch, the Packers' locally generated revenues jumped from about $2 million to $25 million. The last small town standing on the major league horizon had been saved. An exhausted Bob Harlan could breathe again. His big-picture vision had assured financial viability for decades.

Since the refurbishing of Lambeau Field, Green Bay has been the envy of all professional sports. The full force of the Mona Lisa Effect remains visible to this day.

Bob's long-term approach to creating Strategic Drama was eventually translated into a five-story, 376,000-square-foot modern atrium that includes five restaurants, private meeting facilities and luxury boxes. Each year, more than 980 events take place at Lambeau Field—everything from office Christmas parties to corporate retreats, bar mitzvahs to proms and weddings. The Packers now generate about $200 million annually through a wide range of sources such as corporate sponsorships and a well-stocked official Packers pro shop where fans can purchase anything under the sun: player jerseys, caps, hoodies and T-shirts, dog collars and pet clothing, baby crib mobiles, giant foam Cheeseheads, oven mitts, BBQ gear—all adorned with green and gold, the letter "G" and a decent price tag. You can even buy a Packers kitchen toaster that produces the best thing since sliced bread itself: warm, golden brown toast branded with the Packers logo. Don't you love the smell of Green and Gold commerce in the morning?

The crown jewel and most powerful magnet of Harlan's overwhelmingly successful strategy is the Green Bay Packers Hall of Fame. The Packers display their rich and colorful history in vivid fashion with a two-story, 15,000-square-foot museum. Nine galleries feature a treasure trove of more than 80,000 artifacts, along with cutting-edge interactive displays celebrating Packer greats such as Don Hutson, Paul Hornung, Ray Nitschke, Forrest Gregg, Willie Davis and others who scratched and clawed their way through the mud, the dirt and the blood, the glacial ice and blowing snow; running to the daylight of immortality.

The Packers Hall of Fame has more Physical Icons, Energy Boosters, Tangible Symbols and Intangible Rituals than you can imagine. Visitors study everything from Reggie White's game-worn cleats to a rare pin from the Indian Packing Company, along with multiple championship trophies. It's easy to lose yourself and become immersed in the greatest story in sports. The epic underdog tale is showcased in a temple that feels like a sacred inner sanctum as soft, reverent music plays in the background. Like walking through an ancient monastery, people speak in solemn, hushed voices. Grown men are often touched to the point of tearing up.

Take a seat in replica bleachers and watch a film of the famous Ice Bowl, hearing the play-by-play of the last-second block that made offensive guard Jerry Kramer and his bestselling memoir *Instant Replay* a sports literature classic. Pull up a chair and sit at the very desk Vince Lombardi once occupied, situated in a replica office complete with his personal notes, game plans and championship ring. And when the vintage telephone starts buzzing, the commanding voice of the legendary coach himself enthusiastically welcomes you to the home of the *Green Bay Packahs!*

That sound sends a chill down thousands of spines each year.

As the tour continues, you head downstairs to field level, ready to march through the dark stadium tunnel. Accompanied by the same pump-up music and recorded introduction from the stadium P.A. that welcomes the players, you finally set foot on the holy, consecrated ground that is Lambeau Field. Pure sensory overload.

In a heartbeat, you're awash with a surge of Green and Gold pride and energy. You feel the magic of the Packers and their hallowed home.

The spirit of Abundant Generosity is also present, reflected on the Packers Heritage Trail, a free walking, biking and trolley tour featuring 22 landmarks scattered through this one-of-a-kind-town. You learn more about the team's improbable history, with detail as specific as the $2.25 price tag for a season ticket in 1957, the year that Lambeau first opened.

Playing a Different Game

In 1986, religious scholar James Carse of NYU wrote a highly influential book called *Finite and Infinite Games*. Translated into over a dozen languages, the book outlines two radically different approaches to the game of life. Carse was once a player for the NFL's Baltimore Colts, but left football after sustaining a serious knee injury and obtained his PhD through Yale, where he also earned his master of divinity. In his book, Carse argues that *finite* games are defined by known players, fixed rules and agreed-upon objectives that state what victory looks like. From sports to politics to wars, participants obey rules, recognize boundaries and proclaim winners and losers. But, according to Carse, an *infinite* game is completely different.

There are known players, but also some unknown and future contestants. The rules are changeable, fluid and flexible. The objective is entirely different: it is not to win, but to keep playing and extending the game.

Carse metaphorically compares any infinite game to gardening: a successful harvest is not the end of a gardener's existence, but only a phase of it. A garden does not die in the winter. It quietly readies itself for another season.

What happens after you win a finite game? The way Carse sees it, you sign up for another one and showcase past victories. Finite players tend to parade wealth and status, and spend their time in the past, because that's where they were victorious. Infinite players, like Bob Harlan, look to the future. Their goal is to keep the game going. They focus less on the past and devote their energy to figuring out what's possible.

Traditional, finite-thinking business leaders often focus on short-term, limited games, keeping a close eye on numbers and analytics, KPIs and sales results. They frequently speak in a language stuffed with short-term platitudes about their teams being "number one" or "best in class." They often establish arbitrary monthly quotas and fickle financial targets that have no correlation to creating an ethical business or meaningful culture. But, as Carse explains, those who play an infinite game are more focused on making sure the game continues long after they have left.

The Rebirth story of Lambeau Field—and the enduring financial success of the Green Bay Packers—can be directly linked to Bob Harlan's daring vision and his decision to play a longer game. His legacy represents a well-defined model for anyone seeking to become a Big Little Legend in their business category. When financial ruin appeared on the horizon, Bob altered course and set a new direction for his Green and Gold ship. The smallest-market team in all of professional sports has emerged as a consistently high-revenue team with zero debt, a net worth exceeding $2.8 billion and a fanatically loyal customer base. Currently, the season-ticket waiting list counts more than 135,000 people with an estimated wait time of 30 years.

When mothers give birth in the state of Wisconsin, they often add their newborn baby's name to that waiting list in the hopes that one day their family will realize their dream of owning Packers season tickets. In this "publicly owned non-profit corporation," 361,169 people hold a combined 5,009,562 shares. These are non-voting shares, with the last offering in 2011 fetching a price of $250 a share. Technically, the stock has no value. There are no dividends. Shares are not transferable. Much like the Tennessee property that Jack Daniel's bestows upon its fans, Packer backers frame the symbol of their stock certificates to hang proudly in many a man cave. Proceeds are used to fund renovations at historic Lambeau Field to make this place of pilgrimage even more fan friendly. Plenty of big-market clubs in all professional sports leagues are green with envy, wishing they could enjoy the benefits of that much love, moolah and magnetically irresistible attraction.

Bob Harlan brought much more than a winning spirit back to Green Bay, which included two Super Bowl titles during his tenure. He built a sustainable business model with a robust revenue machine that ensures future viability of the franchise and the cathedral called Lambeau Field. Bob's most significant and enduring contribution, however, may be for tens of thousands of business leaders—in any category—who can see the value of a vision that extends far beyond a linear, finite focus on any product, service or profit margins. In the face of a looming financial apocalypse, Bob Harlan recognized that the Packers' greatest asset was its own mystique: a renewable resource and competitive brand advantage that had been neglected and downplayed for about a quarter of a century.

The Green Bay Packers already had the heroes and legends, but they were doing precious little to share their own mythology.

Knowingly or not, Bob employed a story-based playbook similar to legendary brands such as Apple, Disney, Ferrari, Nike and Harley-Davidson. In doing so, he resurrected a franchise that had been left for dead and ensured a continuous flow of legendary stories that would positively impact long-term profitability and fan loyalty for generations to come. Success in such a game, however, can only be played by seeing the world through the lens of irrational idealism.

Like getting clobbered by a jarring clothesline hit from defensive end Willie Davis—who hunted enemy ball carriers during the Lombardi glory years—irrational idealism is a brutal beast.

It has the capacity to defy logic and overpower rational, realistic thinking. Bestselling author Simon Sinek piled on to this trend with a 2019 release called *The Infinite Game*. Building on the earlier work of Carse, Sinek's book forcefully challenges leaders to confront the difficulties of achieving an infinite mindset. According to Sinek, "great leaders are optimistic idealists. They overestimate what we are capable of and inspire us to believe the same."

What if the goal is not just to beat your competition, but to outlast them? As Sinek so eloquently states: "There's no such thing as 'winning' at business. No one is ever declared the winner of business or the winner of careers! There is no winner in marriage. How can you win or be the best in a game that has no finish line?"

It takes real courage, however, to choose ideals and principles over profit. It takes audacity to stand up in a meeting and challenge systems committed to maintaining status quo. When Bob Harlan launched his nine-month mission to restore Lambeau Field and save the Packers, many contemporaries called him crazy. Some even referred to him as a "nut job."

If you are in a boardroom meeting and start talking about the value of Strategic Drama and how it applies to business growth, some people in the room might label you as a kooky, naive idealist who doesn't understand business. Bob Harlan would tell them perhaps they don't know what business game they're playing.

Each day at Lambeau Field, visitors pose for photos ops in the shadows of imposing 14-foot statues of Vince Lombardi and team founder Curly Lambeau. Few are aware, however, of the vital role that Bob Harlan played in executing one of the most remarkable business and brand turnarounds of the 20th century and a foundation for long-term commercial and community success. In 2018, the Packers expanded their business model and brand, turning a 45-acre parcel of land and former eyesore into what is now known as the Titletown District. They are now a real estate company that happens to own an NFL team.

Adjacent to Lambeau Field, the $135 million project opened with amenities such as a full-sized football field, playgrounds, green space and areas for yoga, bocce ball, table tennis, snow tubing and ice skating. Titletown District also includes a brewery, restaurants, upscale hotel, a sports medicine clinic and a business technology incubator. The critical mass created by Titletown has sparked further development: apartment complexes, condominiums, office buildings along with retail, dining and entertainment venues. The Green and Gold should be solidly in the black for many generations to come.

Go Pack Go!

Timeless Takeaways

#1. Time horizon determines longevity.

How far ahead will you peer into the future? Are you ready to plant seeds in fertile ground and grow a forest full of majestic oaks you may never live to see? Average people live in a finite world, stumbling week to week, month to month, paycheck to paycheck. Great leaders like Lincoln, Churchill, FDR, JFK, MLK and Mandela thought in terms of generations. Your ability to see beyond your current time horizon is the key to shaping future socioeconomic success.

Infinite-thinking leaders routinely plant trees that won't bear fruit for months, years or decades. Confident in their vision, they make short-term sacrifices required to shape otherworldly achievements that kick in long after their tenure. Successful leaders don't share this characteristic because they're already rich and can afford the luxury of an expanded time horizon. They *become* successful because they're already playing a much longer game. Average people watch the clock. Leaders watch the calendar.

#2. Brand leadership is an infinite game.

In his 1986 classic, James Carse explained that finite players in any game always play within the boundaries. Infinite players like Bob Harlan compete outside those boundaries, experimenting and re-defining how the game is played.

If you play a finite game, you've likely trained yourself through traditional education to follow the rules. Playing an infinite game, you commit to be becoming a life-long learner and adapting to unknowns. Brand storytelling is a perfect example of an infinite game. There is always something to learn, discern and discover. With skills and craftsmanship, it's possible to craft a timeless Tribal Narrative like Just Do It, Canada's Huggable Car Dealer or Don't Mess With Texas and adapt it to changing conditions. Once your brand develops momentum like bruising Packers fullback Jim Taylor, you can't stop it from crashing over the goal line. It has the power and capacity to Keep Pounding and take on an infinite life of its own.

#3. Never rest on Lambeau laurels.

An extended time horizon and a commitment to storytelling are only the start. Long-term sustainability is only achieved when a leader refuses to settle with present-day conditions. "Never Be Satisfied" is a mindset that demands that there is always a new project to march down the field of life, similar to the way a California rock climber named Yvon has been quarterbacking his brand since 1957.

Starting with a second-hand coal-fired forge, Yvon Chouinard began selling homemade climbing equipment out of the back of his car. In 1970, he expanded into clothing and outdoor gear with a vision of what his company could look like for next "hundred years." He dreamed of creating a business that would inspire a community and do the right thing by the environment along the way. Guided by a greater purpose, he viewed profitability as a by-product of success. From its inception, Patagonia has played a purpose-driven, infinite game. With a core purpose defined as "We're in business to save our home planet," Patagonia continues to be a voice for environmental activism, fighting everything from oil drilling to pipelines, deforestation and governments that deny climate change. Neither Patagonia nor the Green Bay Packers are content to stay where they are, knowing the role they play in creating community and long-term sustainability.

Sudden-Death Overtime

The Green Bay Packers are just one example of the many organizations that have established brand identities that go far beyond the actual products, services or events being sold. They embody an infinite way of looking at the world similar to what Steve Jobs envisioned January 9, 2007, when he unveiled the iPhone at the annual Macworld gathering in San Francisco. Wearing his trademark Levis and black turtleneck, Jobs told the crowd of 4,000, "We're going to make history today. Apple is going to reinvent the phone. A leapfrog product that is way smarter than any mobile device has ever been and super easy to use."

Looking back, we know Jobs was right. The iPhone became one of the most iconic products in consumer electronics history as much as five years ahead of any other provider at the time. Jobs thought it would be a success if Apple could capture even 1% market share of the mobile market in 2008, which converts to 10 million iPhones.

Apple beat that 10 million goal by September 2008—three months ahead of schedule. In July 2016, Apple announced it had sold 1 billion iPhones. By August of 2020, Apple became the first U.S. company to be valued at $2 trillion, reaching the milestone just two years after becoming the world's first trillion-dollar company in 2018. History has produced a long line of idealistic romantics who conceptualized their own infinite field of dreams, dating back to Galileo, Da Vinci, Newton, Einstein, Edison and Earhart. Similar torches have been carried into the business world by Steve Jobs, Yvon Chouinard and Big Little Legends like Bob Harlan, revealing how mere mortals can also imagine and implement breakthrough ideas that tilt the playing field.

Creating a magnetically irresistible brand that accumulates reputational equity begins with a clear, courageous vision that refuses to accept "what is" and explores instead "what can be." It's an utter refusal to settle for realistic outcomes or blindly follow factual data. It's about asking unrealistic and idealistic questions such as: "What conditions need to be in place in order for us to win a game of our own creation on our own frozen field of dreams?"

Bob Harlan stepped down following the 2007 season and has since been inducted into the Packers Hall of Fame. Fittingly, the area in front of the cavernous Lambeau Field atrium has been named in his honor. The Robert E. Harlan Plaza occupies a permanent place alongside the statues of Curly Lambeau and Vince Lombardi. Brilliant, "big picture" infinite thinking might well be Bob's most enduring legacy, exemplifying how an everyday leader can transform a brand. He put the Green Bay Packers on a sustainable path that took a small-town company light-years away from relying on ten events a year to make payroll, keep the lights on, the grass mowed and stadium doors open.

No leader can afford to coast on credentials, status or past accomplishments. It's a terrible feeling when you wake up one day and realize you've become out-of-step and obsolete. Leaders respect the need to plant trees long before they need the shade. To repair systems before they break and renew business models and brands before they get punted into irrelevance.

True visionaries bridge the gap between present-day reality and Green and Gold possibilities.

They know idealism beats the frozen snot out of realism.

How far out will you start projecting your unrealistic future? Can you envision a business and brand that will outlast your involvement?

If they start calling you crazy, consider it a compliment.

And think of Bob Harlan.

The measure of who we are
is what we do with what we have.

VINCE LOMBARDI

12

THE FAIRWAY TO HEAVEN

An Old Course to Find Your Original Story

July 9, 1960

Scotland.

A rich cultural tapestry of colorful kilts. Lusty bagpipes. Spicy haggis. Potent whisky.

Look around every corner of the country and you'll discover a legend. Majestic Edinburgh Castle. The mystery of Loch Ness. William Wallace; Robert the Bruce; Robbie Burns; Mary, Queen of Scots.

First among those legends is the birthplace of golf. The Old Course at St Andrews. Dating back to the 15th-century Kingdom of Fife, this hallowed, par-72 layout is, for golfers, the metaphorical equivalent to Bethlehem, Mecca and the Vatican all rolled up into one. This is sacred and holy ground. Old Tom Morris, Bobby Jones, Ben Hogan, Jack Nicklaus, Tiger Woods and many others have struggled mightily to master this temperamental, tempestuous, awe-inspiring 7,305 yards of windswept links nestled on the North Sea Coast. Presidents, prime ministers and everyday people have their own horror stories of being trapped in Hell Bunker on 14. Flirting with disaster on the daunting Road Hole on 17. Traversing iconic Swilcan Bridge and taking that ethereal walk along the 18th fairway; arriving at a green that sits quietly in the shadows of the imposing Royal & Ancient Clubhouse.

This is where Jimmy grew up and learned the game.

Jimmy left town in the late 1950s, but the legacy of St Andrews has never left him.

Everybody in the small community of 11,000 knew his face from the articles that kept appearing in the newspapers. Folks in pubs would say "Jimmy is going places" after yet another story in the sports section about his latest exploits. By the age of 17, the young champion had amassed boxes full of trophies and a scrapbook of press clippings confirming his status as one of Scotland's most promising and talented golfers.

On Christmas Day 1956, a letter arrived in the post from Canada extending an offer for the teenager to turn professional.

By April of '57, Jimmy was on a propeller plane out of Prestwick and headed across the Atlantic to make a full-time living playing the game he had loved since first picking up a club at the age of seven.

On the U.K. passport he held, his full name read James Gair Maxwell. Listed as his birthday was the same date that Canada declared war against Nazi Germany: September 10, 1939.

Jimmy is my father.

He is the reason I write about legends.

Take the Long Way Home

Name something that is both deceptively simple and end-lessly complicated. A parallel journey with finite beginnings and endings that reveals how you can deal with failure and achieve infinite success. Answer with either one of two four-letter words and you will be correct.

"L-I-F-E" or "G-O-L-F."

Following his relocation to Canada, Dad became assistant pro at the Lambton Golf and Country Club in Toronto before meeting my mother and settling into life as a husband, father and competitive athlete in New Brunswick. His résumé includes over 100 victories at local and regional tournaments, multiple course records, several provincial titles and enshrinement in a number of sports halls of fame. In every sense of the word, Dad exemplified the many virtues his sport has to offer.

- Never late for a tee time.

- Never a curse word or thrown club after a missed shot.

- Never blaming anyone but himself for a lousy round.

- Always in control of his emotions in the heat of battle.

- Always respectful of his opponents as well as of the rules, traditions and spirit of the game.

- Always working to improve his shot-making ability.

Jimmy's boyhood hero, the legendary Bobby Jones, was once quoted as saying, "Golf is the closest game to the game we call life. You get bad breaks from good shots, good breaks from bad shots—but you have to play where it lies."

In many respects, golf is a lot like the mental discipline required for long-term brand building. You need to prepare and work hard. Hope to have a little luck along the way. And then, one day, you might beat the course, get noticed and win.

My father was born seven minutes from the first tee at St Andrews, but he easily recalls those days in the '40s and '50s when The Old Course wasn't globally famous. Only a few scattered tourists would show up. No tee times were being booked a year in advance. It was hardly the bucket list destination that now attracts hundreds of thousands each year. But three years after Dad left his boyhood home, one man and a small army changed all that. An American man who refused to play it safe and follow the crowd.

On and off the course, Arnold marched to his own beat. Without him, The Old Course—and the entire sport of golf—would never have become a global force to be reckoned with. In the years that followed World War II, few American pro golfers ventured across the pond. Travel was long and arduous. Prize money was a pittance. The idiosyncrasies of links golf were frustrating. For a touring American pro, a trip to Great Britain was a money-losing, time-sucking, out-of-pocket proposition offering little or no enjoyment.

Arnold chose to see things differently.

Growing up next door to a golf course in Latrobe, Pennsylvania, Arnold Palmer was a student of the game. He had read all about Bobby Jones's historic Grand Slam of 1930—winning the U.S. and British Opens and the U.S. and British Amateurs—a feat that has never been matched. In 1960, he and a Pittsburgh sportswriter hatched the idea of creating a professional Grand Slam—the two Opens, the Masters and the PGA Championship. He believed that packaging these four events would bring more attention, allure and majesty to the sport. More attention would inspire more fans to fall in love with the game, which, in turn, would attract more media coverage, sponsors, prize money and potential earnings.

For his Grand Slam concept to have substance, though, Palmer needed to compete in the British Open. He needed to follow through and take action.

That year, while his U.S. counterparts stayed home, Arnold Palmer arrived in Scotland on a rampage. With 19 Tour victories, including three major championships already under his belt, 1960 was Palmer's year. After winning the Masters during a televised event at Augusta in April, he came back from being down seven shots to win the U.S. Open, beating Nicklaus by two shots at Cherry Hills. Now he had his sights set on the third leg of the new Grand Slam he envisioned. With golf's star attraction making his first trip to the U.K., prize money for the British Open went up 40%. British fans—even non-golfers—were excited to see what the charismatic yet humble American would bring to the tournament. A Pennsylvania steel town kid, Palmer had an unparalleled combination of approachable and down-to-earth fused with competitive bravado. Never one to play conservative and layup, Palmer displayed an aggressive, grip-it and rip-it style with a slashing, attacking swing. Men admired him. Women adored him.

Mass media fanned the hype. Hordes of reporters and television cameras saw history unfold. Stories of the colorful

Palmer and his reverential admiration for The Old Course and what it symbolized were splashed in newspapers on both sides of the Atlantic. With millions reading local papers and watching on TV, Palmer singlehandedly put a forgotten St Andrews on the global map. Backed by an enormous gallery of fans dubbed "Arnie's Army," Palmer served up plenty of drama on the final round, July 9, 1960. Down by four shots with nine holes to play, he fired a couple of birdies, made par on the Road Hole at 17 and birdied 18 only to lose by a single stroke to Australian Kel Nagle.

When Arnold Palmer finished runner-up at the 1960 British Open, it ended his Grand Slam bid. The story, however, endures to this day. Through Jack Nicklaus. Through Tiger Woods. Through every current superstar and every British Open contested at St Andrews. Palmer emerged as golf's first celebrity of the television age and, in paying homage to The Old Course and the legends who came before him, he sparked worldwide fascination in "The Home of Golf." From that day forward, St Andrews would be regarded as the penultimate pantheon of the sport. Palmer would certify its legacy on multiple return visits before an emotional farewell on Swilcan Bridge in 1995.

Stories don't end.

Sometimes, you're just not sure where they begin. Which explains why the Mona Lisa Effect still impacts The Old Course to this day.

An Old Course on Building Legends

According to the Royal & Ancient, there were 38,864 golf courses in the world as of 2020. Only three of those are regarded as must-play destinations on every golfer's bucket list: California's Pebble Beach, Georgia's Augusta National and Scotland's Old Course at St Andrews. Whether it's the number of golf courses globally or the 35,000-plus paintings that hang in a Paris museum, the metaphor still applies for anyone aiming to achieve top-of-mind awareness while competing in an overcrowded, competitive marketplace. The Home of Golf, Leonardo's *Mona Lisa* and the many small companies explored in this book all illustrate how the power of storytelling can dramatically alter the fortunes of any person, place, organization or object. How a compelling saga holds the potential to inspire deeply emotional, even biochemically infused responses from otherwise normal humans—and to extend that effect over centuries.

Nursing a frosty pint in a noisy Scottish pub called the Dunvegan, you lean in and listen to a retired IBM executive admit how emotional he felt during his first time at The Old Course. Murray confesses to feeling "verklempt"—a Yiddish word that describes being so choked up so as to be unable to speak. Listening to him speak, it's clear that sentimentality doesn't often mix into the daily life of this detail-oriented, by-the-book, Colorado businessman. Nevertheless, Murray is just one of tens of thousands who will go out of their way to cross mighty oceans, pay top dollar and invest oodles of time for the privilege of experiencing the perceptual reality of walking with history.

Queues for the few public slots available each day begin forming outside the starters building at the Old Pavilion at 3:30 a.m. Raving fans and global ambassadors purchase nearly $20 million of ancillary St Andrews clothing, souvenirs and branded merchandise each year, often framing them to pass down for generations.

The ripple effect from Arnold Palmer's momentous 1960 visit to The Old Course drove popularity of the sport to new heights. It awakened the entire planet to the historical significance of the origins of the game. Palmer opened the floodgates for every touring pro to pursue the mythical Grand Slam and compete in the British Open. He inspired men, women and children the world over to pick up a club and learn how to play golf.

Golf journalist and eight-time Canadian women's long drive champion Lisa Vlooswyk of Calgary, Alberta, was on a 2002 golfing trip with her husband to the famed Pebble Beach course when, lo and behold, they encountered a gracious Palmer on the first tee. After a giddy photo op, the couple watched in awe as Arnie ripped his driver straight down the pipe. Recalling the moment and knowing her golf history, Vlooswyk says today that "Arnold Palmer not only inspired dads to bring sons and daughters to the golf course, his legend also lives on through moms. Mothers and grandmothers are now sharing their joy of the game with the next generation, which is why I introduced my son to the sport. No wonder Mr. Palmer is still the King!"

Away from the course, Arnold Palmer is a classic prototype that any leader can study and learn from for the way he developed his business and brand acumen. He was the first in his sport to understand how favorable attention generated through fans and media could be converted into commercial opportunities. He implicitly understood—no different from today—that attention equals currency.

Palmer was the original client for IMG (International Management Group), one of the world's premiere sports and talent agencies. On a handshake deal, Arnie and Mark McCormack—the undisputed king of sports marketing—worked to invent a formula to make more money off the golf course than on it. Long before Michael Jordan, Tiger Woods, LeBron James or Serena Williams signed nine-figure Nike contracts, Arnold Palmer paved the way with an irresistible business model and brand. It certainly helped that he was handsome and talented, with a virile, swashbuckling image and credentials that included 62 PGA wins and seven major championships. But Palmer and McCormack shared a much bigger vision for what they could generate in commercial impact and potential revenues that extended far beyond any tournament purse.

Starting with a car commercial for Cadillac, Palmer's golden touch as a pitchman boosted bottom lines for multiple brands: Rolex, Pennzoil, Hertz, Mastercard, Callaway, AriZona Beverages and many others. He and McCormack launched a global apparel brand, created the Arnold Palmer Design Company and its more than 300 signature courses in 23 countries, and, in 1995, helped launch the Golf Channel, America's first single-sport cable network. *Forbes* estimates that, over 52 years as a professional golfer, Palmer won $3.6 million as a player. Off the course, the magazine pegged his lifetime earnings at the time of his passing in 2016 at

$875 million. Together, Palmer and McCormack transformed celebrity endorsement from a novelty to a highly impactful and lucrative industry. In effect, they created the template for the entire celebrity endorsement business still followed to this day. No town was beyond the reach of his brand, with a network of Arnold Palmer Mini-Putt golf courses spreading across the U.K. and North America, including a location in my hometown of Moncton, New Brunswick, next to our city's first McDonald's on Mountain Road.

Arnold Palmer was one of the original "influencer marketers." The tide that lifted all boats. He left The Old Course—along with the British Open, an entire sport, dozens of well-known brands and himself, McCormack and IMG—awash with prosperity. By tapping into the legacy of St Andrews while harnessing the emerging power of television, Palmer tilted the earth on its axis. Only 8% of American households had televisions in 1950. A decade later, that number was nearly 90%. For Palmer, 1960 was the year all the stars aligned. Victories at the Masters, the U.S. Open, the McCormack partnership, his inaugural trip to Scotland and a gallant second-place finish at the Home of Golf in the midst of television's cultural earthquake, all forever documented to be remembered by an adoring press and public.

When Dad won the Nova Scotia Open at Lingan in 1961, he pocketed the top prize money of $250. Successfully defending that crown a year later in Amherst, he also won $250. Looking back, it's easy to see that, in the late '50s and early '60s, golf wasn't a game that would make my father or any professional rich or famous.

Until Arnold Palmer came along.

Timing, as they say, is everything.

From a leadership perspective, it's crucial to recognize the role you play in recognizing when the time is right. When the opportunity presents itself to build a bridge that connects the past to your future.

Even if it means declaring war on another country.

No Way Norway!

Over the course of this book, you've heard about leaders of small- to mid-sized organizations who assumed the mantle of responsibility for getting their brands noticed and ensuring future prosperity. To offer something worthy of attention and rally people around a larger idea. Here is their lesson in a nutshell: you may not have a massive marketing budget to compete with the bigger players, but somehow you have got to find a way if you don't want the ship you are sailing to run aground, or worse, sink into the ocean of irrelevance. It's your job to make a splash. But how?

That's what Fraser was wondering as he sat in on a TEC Canada executive session in Regina, Saskatchewan, on June 8, 2018. Listening to a guest speaker, he began visualizing a new blue-sky future for his small-town brand. He immediately recognized that the timing was perfect. Like Bob Harlan, he could picture his organization setting itself miles apart from all others in the quest to boost tourism, attract outside investment and keep a community growing. Following that session, Fraser thrust a business card into my hand.

Before dashing off to another meeting, he exclaimed, "We gotta talk! This is exactly what we need to do!"

Within a week, Mayor Fraser Tolmie confirmed plans to host a one-day branding bootcamp for about 25 business and civic leaders in his community. Elected as mayor in 2016, the former pilot who had flown F-18s with the Royal Canadian Air Force was concerned with signs of dwindling civic pride and economic stagnation. With his town's population hovering at the 34,000 mark for nearly 20 years, Fraser knew the time was ripe for drastic change and a new direction. He didn't want to see his city shrivel and shrink, as so many other small towns had.

Other than its unique name, there was nothing outwardly remarkable about Moose Jaw, Saskatchewan. Their marketing brochures and civic website made the same promises as every other municipality: a great place to live, work and play, with clean water, low taxes, plenty of shopping, good schools and friendly neighborhoods. The entire category essentially speaks the same language—all paraphrased as "quality of life." And while the facts may be true, this approach makes it impossible for outside investors or tourists to distinguish one friendly, welcoming town from another.

You can't grow a brand identity until you know it. And at some point during that day-long bootcamp in September 2018, Tolmie suddenly realized he *did* know it. A history lesson that had been lying dormant for decades. One of the strangest, most out-of-the-ordinary stories in Canadian history.

During the Prohibition Era of the 1920s, Moose Jaw earned a racy reputation as one of the wildest frontier towns in the West. The little town in the middle of the prairies had plenty of gambling, drinking, bootlegging and loose women. Illegal activities thrived here in part due to a network of tunnels hidden beneath the downtown streets—an ideal hideout for mobsters, madams, illegal immigrants and rum runners. With a railway terminus on the Soo line direct from Chicago, Moose Jaw offered a perfect escape route for gangsters like "Public Enemy #1" Al Capone when they needed to lay low from time to time. For decades, elderly southern Saskatchewan farmers told stories of how Moose Jaw was known as "Little Chicago," with tales of bulletproofed cars doing cross-border booze runs. People gossiped about bumping into Capone at the barber shop, enjoying small talk with "Scarface" and his scary, pistol-packing second-in-command, "Diamond" Jim Brady.

For many God-fearing, hard-working citizens of Moose Jaw, being known as a gangster's paradise was not something to be proud of. City officials denied rumors of secret tunnels—until 1985, when a manhole collapsed over Main Street and exposed a large, brick-lined subterranean network. Moose Jaw's dirty little secret was now out in the open. The "Tunnels of Moose Jaw" have since been restored as a year-round tourist attraction, but the town's checkered history also provided valuable pieces of what would eventually become its entire brand strategy.

What if we decided to embrace this sketchy, unsavory past?

After that September 2018 seminar, Tolmie and his team made sure Moose Jaw would forever and legitimately be established as distinctively different from every other community in North America. In a way that can never be replicated, they staked their claim as "Canada's Most Notorious City."

The first shot was fired on Friday, January 11, 2019.

Saskatchewan's favorite social media rock stars, "Justin and Greg," did a little research and uncovered an international travesty that demanded public attention. A scandal that needed to be brought to light. The plucky pair discovered that, four years earlier, a town in Norway had dared to erect a moose statue 30 centimeters higher than Moose Jaw's own "Mac the Moose," thus relegating the Canadian icon to #2 in the world. In righteous mock indignation, Justin and Greg shot a video in front of Mac the Moose, throwing down a patriotic gauntlet and insisting that Mayor Tolmie take retaliatory action.

Publicly, they demanded that Fraser use all the powers at his disposal to answer this most egregious offense. "We are calling on the mayor of Moose Jaw to find a way to put 31 centimeters back on Mac and stick it to Norway!" they shouted in pseudo seriousness on their 79-second Facebook video. That weekend, the video generated 150,000-plus views, along with more than 500 shares and comments. The story was spreading like a prairie brush fire. The mayor was being forced to take a stand.

Now it was Fraser's turn to put up or shut up.

How would he answer the bell and respond to this challenge? Would he fold his cards and, like so many politicians, artfully dodge the question?

Or would he drop his gloves and come out swinging?

Within 48 hours, Fraser tossed gasoline on the social media blaze. Drawing a line in the snow, he defiantly stood in front of Mac the Moose and delivered his own smack-talk YouTube video. He vowed revenge on the rural town of Stor-Elvdal, which had the audacity to steal away the title of the world's tallest moose statue. The mayor issued a call to arms for all Canadians to fight back. Within a few days, the father of two daughters was on national news, declaring that the war had become personal. Deadpanning for the cameras, he said, "Don't tell us we can't put maple syrup on our pancakes. Don't water down our beer. Don't tell us *Hockey Night in Canada* is a chat show. And whether it's Norway or any country on the planet, don't mess with Mac the Moose!"

Overnight, the publicity snowball became an unstoppable avalanche. Moose Jaw was attracting worldwide attention comparable to what was showered on the theft of the *Mona Lisa* in 1911 and The Old Course in 1960. Fraser was being interviewed 15 to 20 times a day, with coverage from the *New York Times*, CNN, BBC World Service, CBC's *The National*, the *Washington Post*, Virgin Radio and the *South China Morning Post*. The story reached a fever pitch with a four-minute feature on *The Late Show with Stephen Colbert*.

Rival musicians even jumped on board. A Norwegian duo extended an olive branch with a "Moose Truce" dance music video, encouraging Canadians to find resolution. Halifax-based songwriter Dave Carroll, who went viral with "United Breaks Guitars" in 2009 (now also a book), would have none of that. The satirical Carroll responded with "No Way Norway!"—a jaunty yet defiant little ditty declaring that Moose Jaw and all of Canada would never back down.

Friendly no more.

Mr. Nice Guy had caught the last train to Chicago.

For a quiet community looking to shake things up, this international war of words represented a bonanza of tens of millions of dollars of free publicity, a marketing success story that no amount of money could buy. A GoFundMe page was set up to support the non-profit restoration of Mac the Moose and a flood of donations followed, including contributions from the Vegas Golden Knights NHL team and a $25,000 check from Moosehead Breweries.

When the snow finally began to melt in March, so did the heated words. It was time for peace talks.

After two months of intercontinental conflict, the heads of these two warring townships gathered for the world's first "Moose Summit." They signed an official treaty and issued a joint communiqué declaring a spirit of détente that ended Cold War II. Social media guns fell silent. There were no more digital broadsides as Fraser Tolmie and Stor-Elvdal Deputy Mayor Linda Otnes Henriksen buried the hatchet. Before cameras and onlookers, the two mayors affixed signatures to an official "Moose Truce," sealed with a document dubbed a "Moosarandum of Understanding." The *Washington Post* published the historic accord, in which both sides made concessions and agreed to future friendship, discussion and mutual cooperation.

> Moose Jaw's statue, known as "Mac the Moose," currently 32 feet, will reclaim the title of tallest moose in the world, pending cosmetic enhancement of his antlers. Stor-Elvdal's, "Storelgen," which is a 33-foot silver fox of a moose, will "forevermore be known as the shiniest and most attractive Moose in the world."

With the dignitaries shaking hands before their respective national flags, the end of the friendly feud between a Saskatchewan prairie town and a Scandinavian municipality further reinforced the brand strategy that was already underway to create "Canada's Most Notorious City." Looking back, Fraser Tolmie, the only son of Scottish immigrants from Glasgow pointed out, "Once we knew our identity, only then could we embrace our destiny."

Walking with Destiny

When Arnold Palmer crossed Swilcan Bridge and headed up the 18th fairway on July 9, 1960, he ushered in waves of economic, social and cultural prosperity that are now valued in the billions. Amplified by the platform of television, his bold and somewhat risky move to travel to Scotland that year represents the risk that any legacy-minded leader must take. Likewise, Fraser Tolmie gambled on himself and on the small army backing him, daring to look the camera in the eye and influence millions while leveraging platforms such as Facebook and YouTube. If they were sharing a pint in a Scottish pub, Arnie and Fraser would nod and agree as fellow pilots and golfers that the journey of a thousand miles always begins with a first, uncertain step. To create a timeless legend, you have start by building a bridge that links your past with your future.

Just as Palmer's overseas junket and the narrative of the Quest that had him making his journey to St Andrews had affected the global golf community, Fraser's small town also reaped enormous, never-ending rewards from discovering, telling and living their own story. In 2019 alone, tourism skyrocketed by more than 30%. Outside investment has escalated. They've won multiple marketing awards from the Economic Developers Association of Canada.

Thinking less like a municipality and more like their own media company, the City of Moose Jaw, Saskatchewan, is now a model for what it takes to attract global attention, earn millions in free publicity, restore civic pride, inspire a sustainable surge in tourism and boost economic development. At the height of the 2020 pandemic, "Canada's Most Notorious City" gained even more traction with a series of videos featuring exchanges between the mayor and Jon Hamm, a.k.a. Don Draper of *Mad Men* fame. In February 2021, Fraser Tolmie appeared poolside at Temple Gardens Hotel & Spa, wearing only a pristine bathrobe and poking fun at Canadian politicians who had selfishly bolted for sunny destinations over the Christmas holidays while telling their constituents to stay home and self-isolate.

Removing cucumber slices from his eyes, the mock serious mayor asked, "Are you a Canadian politician taking heat for going away at Christmas? I'm notoriously lucky, because I don't need to take the heat to get away from it all." Champagne in hand, Tolmie paused to take a bite of a juicy strawberry before offering this tongue-in-cheek advice: "If you're someone trying to escape from it all, do what Al Capone did. Come to Canada's Most Notorious City. We'll never tell."

Once again, the social media universe responded heavily in Moose Jaw's favor. Millions of subsequent impressions and a renewed avalanche of press attention served to support the city's long-term strategy and furthered its potential to build reputational equity for generations. Reaching back into their colorful past, Moose Jaw took bold, confident steps into the future, packing its unique character and qualities into a dramatic, four-word Tribal Narrative. By thinking beyond the basic marketing table stakes, Moose Jaw played a more infinite game as local leaders recognized their role in creating the Strategic Drama that perfectly encapsulated their distinctive civic story. Aligned with at least four of the *The Seven Basic Plots*, including Comedy, Voyage & Return, Rebirth and Overcoming the Monster, Moose Jaw also leveraged its forgotten Physical Icon and gave Mac the Moose new life after a successful and much publicized "antlerectomy" and the later grafting of a new, taller rack in September 2019. The strategy also sparked a number of new Tangible Symbols and Intangible Rituals, with "notorious" merchandise, branded street banners throughout the downtown and local companies like Little Chicago Entertainment hopping on the brandwagon with a 1920s speakeasy and mobster-themed adventure rooms.

These success stories don't happen, however, unless a leader like Arnold Palmer or Fraser Tolmie decides to put their personal and professional reputation on the line. Anyone can sit back and admire the story of the little guy taking on the world and winning against all odds. But if Arnie and Fraser were back together at the Dunvegan again, they would confirm there are always moments of self-doubt— those persistent, nagging voices inside your head that keep insisting you're going to fail or make yourself look silly. But silencing that inner critic is the job every leader signs up for.

To step up to that metaphorical first tee at The Old Course in St Andrews. To hear the starter announce your name. To grab the driver in your bag and, in full public view, take your best swing. Always hoping the ball lands somewhere down the middle of the fairway.

Michael Dubin. Jim and Dawna Gilbert. Rick Harrison. John Yokoyama. Paul Weber Sr. Tom Rennie. Barb Stegemann. Rachel Mielkie. Casey Neistat. Jesse Cole. Bill Bowerman. Roy and Pennie Williams. Bob Harlan. Fraser Tolmie and all the Big Little Legends in this book share a common thread and a similar mindset. They share a belief in an idea that so strong they're prepared to cross oceans and go for broke with no guarantee of success. To pull swords from stones, to plant flags on their own mountain of values—and to die with their boots on.

Timeless Takeaways

#1. Find the buried lies.

A fervent student of golf history, Arnold Palmer paid close attention to the accomplishments of Bobby Jones and the significant role played by St Andrews in his 1930 Grand Slam. The second American after Ben Franklin to be conferred with Freedom of the City honors by the Town of St Andrews in 1958, Jones was in the final throes of a crippling ailment when he delivered a moving speech before a crowd of 1,700 at Graduation Hall. Battling back tears, Jones stated, "I could take out of my life everything but my experiences here in St Andrews and I would still have had a rich and full life."

Palmer's 1960 trip to the British Open not only honored the tournament and The Old Course but also the legacy of the sport's greatest athlete at that time. Without any formal plan, Arnie knew the financial future and prosperity of his sport lay buried in the past.

Decades later, the City of Moose Jaw, Saskatchewan, dug through the dusty archives of its dubious history and unearthed golden trunks of storytelling treasures that could drive its brand forward and make a mark for generations. Whether your story is one of dignity, honor and heritage or something that comes with a shady past, the key is recognizing a subject worthy of fascination.

#2. Reinvent "the game."

Average or mediocre performers in any field of human endeavor tend to bellyache about "the game"—all those constraints, rules, playing conditions, competitors and more. They point fingers at the economy, the weather, the media, the government, society, long-haired hippies, heavy metal music, millennials or the latest technology. They grumble and protest about how life and business should be "fair."

Legends take responsibility for reinventing whatever game they're playing. They tilt playing fields to their advantage while striving to make everything better for the greater good—including opponents they may compete against one day. Like any pro golfer knows about their game, they know that life and business is inherently and eternally unfair. Instead of complaining, they invest thousands of hours into honing their skills so that they're prepared for those rare moments of great opportunity. They see beyond the present, make tough decisions and strike when irons of opportunity are smoking hot—all while adapting and adjusting to changing market conditions.

#3. Who's your caddy?

The great British golf writer Henry Longhurst once said: "A good caddy is more than a mere assistant. He is a guide, philosopher and friend." A great caddy is a trusted teammate and strategist who sees things the pro golfer cannot. Stance. Rhythm. Tempo. Temperament. Besides carrying your clubs, a top-notch caddy will check yardages, identify ideal targets and "danger" areas to avoid, map the slopes and breaks of the green, the prevailing winds and more, all to help their players make better, more informed decisions. Essentially, a top-notch caddy provides a unique perspective that addresses this question: "How can you read the label when you are stuck inside the bottle?"

In business and life, everyone exists within their own bottle. CEOs, sales managers, HR types, front-line supervisors, athletes, artists, academics, tech support, cashiers, mechanics and more all operate within their own orientation and perspective. Leaders, however, take pains to ensure their current perspective does not become a myopic liability. They reach out and consult a trusted advisor or coach who can see threats and opportunities they can't. Arnold Palmer needed "outside the bottle" help from Ohio lawyer Mark McCormack to re-imagine the entire professional golf tour from a business and brand point of view. Mayor

Fraser Tolmie did much the same thing when he gathered civic leaders and invited an outside consultant to facilitate a process to re-examine the Moose Jaw brand from top to bottom. Some bottles have lids screwed on so tightly that they prevent us from climbing out and seeing what's on the outside. Frequently, the biggest lies are the ones we tell ourselves about who wrote the label on our bottle in the first place. Was it us, or somebody else? A different set of eyes can help you understand your own role in a situation, and take better aim with your next shot. Business, life and golf are hard enough. Great coaches and caddies can trim a few strokes off anyone's scorecard.

The 19th Hole

Arnold Palmer may not go down as the greatest golfer in history. That distinction may belong to Old Tom Morris, Bobby Jones, Sam Snead, Ben Hogan, Jack Nicklaus or Tiger Woods, or to someone else entirely.

The humble son of a greenskeeper from Latrobe, Pennsylvania, will always be remembered, however, as one of the world's best citizens: one with strength of mind, integrity and character. Palmer built a rich legacy of philanthropic efforts that include the Arnie's Army Charitable Foundation and the Arnold Palmer Hospital for Children in Orlando. Nicknamed "The King," he showed a spirit of Abundant Generosity that forever altered his sport and the many people and causes he touched. He was appreciative of his fans, and selflessly shook every hand and signed autographs for hours. A true pioneer, Palmer singlehandedly took golf out of its snooty, upscale country clubs and elevated it to the mainstream without ever losing his common touch.

Palmer was born on September 10, 1929. Born on the same day, exactly ten years apart, my own father displayed many of those same personal qualities while serving as a teaching pro on Canada's east coast.

Jimmy transferred his love of the game to thousands of boys and girls anxious to learn the techniques of a sport that represents so much more than just smacking a golf ball over 300 yards and draining 80-foot putts. What golf can teach about genuine humility and strength of character is just as relevant for any business leader who aspires to create their own legacy. With golf as his classroom, Dad taught many life lessons. Let your work do the talking. The work never really ends. A real pro constantly prepares, practices and does it again tomorrow.

The best musicians play endless scales. The best actors constantly rehearse in front of bedroom mirrors. The best authors endlessly write, research, edit and re-write. The best golfers, like Arnie and Jimmy, invest countless lonely hours on practice greens and driving ranges to perfect their skills.

Away from the spotlight. Working their craft. For a game that can't be won—only played.

On an endless quest to find their true, authentic swing.

In his 1995 novel *The Legend of Bagger Vance*, author Steven Pressfield introduces us to a former golf hero who has lost his swing. Crushed by hardships and tragedies, the troubled WWI veteran surrenders to his inner demons. Gives up the sport. Walks away from the game he once loved. A decade later, the reluctant local kid gets a second chance with an exhibition match in his hometown of Savannah, featuring golf titans Walter Hagen and Bobby Jones and offering a purse of $20,000. In his gripping tale, Pressfield weaves together a powerful underlying message of the struggle between the True Self and the Ego—a conflict every golfer knows only too well. His central premise is that our true authentic swing is already within us: a message conveyed by mysterious mentor and caddy Bagger Vance, who reminds the hero—and you, the reader—that our authentic swing is remembered, not learned. It's the swing only you can make. Inscribed into your DNA. The metaphorical "sweet spot" that represents the story you entered this world with.

If you can discover it, tell it and, more importantly, live it, that swing—that story—is the source code for your own unique legend. It's where you can discover your own Mona Lisa Effect, always waiting patiently for you. All you have to do is pick up a club and step up to the tee.

Like the purest golf swing that lands an approach shot less than three feet from the flag, your story can take you exactly where you want to be.

My father discovered his early. His swing—his *story*—was equally metaphorical and literal. At the age of 82, he was still walking and playing 18 without a power cart. When asked what his sport means to him, my father responded with this: "Golf has done a world of good for me. I've seen a lot of Canada and been on three Willingdon Cup teams. It's taught me valuable lessons in self-reliance and personal integrity. No teammates can bail you out. You can't blame referees. Your outcomes are based solely on your decisions and only you know if you're cheating." Jimmy had no idea what adventures were in store when he left Scotland at 17, but he is eternally grateful for both the sport and its lessons, saying, "It's a simple game. It's just you against the golf course while facing your own fears and battling your own insecurities. For 99% of the time, the golf course wins, but, every now and then, with a lot of hard work and a little bit of luck, you come out on top and experience a feeling like no other."

Jimmy was on the receiving end of a little bit of luck during his career. Besides his many honors and recording six holes-in-one, he was fortunate enough to compete in one of sport's rarest statistical oddities. My father may be the only professional golfer in history to have participated in a four-generational foursome in three consecutive years. In August 2019, September 2020 and August 2021, Jimmy played fully competitive rounds of 18 alongside his son, his grandson Ryan and his great-grandson Cayden, who, at age 13, showed great promise, with many 220-yard drives straight down the middle. Beyond our immediate family and all who know and admire him, Jim Maxwell from St Andrews, Scotland, is his own Big Little Legend.

As a leader, building an enduring, irresistible brand means finding that one unique swing—it means digging down to uncover the single story that is authentically true and only yours. How that brand story is told—and how it might trigger your own Mona Lisa Effect—is a question only you can answer. Through the course of this book, you have discovered that long-term brand building is its own discipline, driven by leaders who invest in ideas that aren't sure things; leaders who make bigger, bolder decisions with a braver point of view. No guarantees. Running toward risk, not away from it.

Yes, there are two paths you can take, but there's always time to change the road you're on. Legendary brands can only be built by leaders—not by marketing companies or consultants. Legends fully embrace Strategic Drama and ride the razor's edge. They're never afraid to go for broke or carry the water and they don't follow the same marketing rules as everybody else.

You don't have to follow those rules either.

Will your shadow be taller than your soul?

From Amelia Earhart to Led Zeppelin, legends break and take new ground.

They are people a lot like you, who choose roads less traveled.

If we're on this earth to find meaning in our lives, careers, communities and games we play, what is the timeless narrative that explains the road you are on? For Jim and Dawna Gilbert, it is the story of love: for their customers, their employees and their community. For the City of Moose Jaw, it is relishing the story of a crooked, notorious past.

For my father, his story is a lifetime of reflection on the ups, downs and eternal links between life, business and golf. "You can always do better. Don't ever give up. The most important shot is the next one. It's about living in the moment and never looking back."

Words well said for any leader who hopes to hit it long and straight along the lush, heavenly fairways of any well-played life.

*This is the origin of the game,
golf in its purest form, and it's still played
that way on an Old Course seemingly
untouched by time. Every time I play here,
it reminds me that this is still a game.*

ARNOLD PALMER

SOURCES & ACKNOWLEDGMENTS

THE CONCEPT FOR this book was born following a speaking engagement on April 24, 2018, at the legendary Torrey Pines Golf Course, just north of San Diego. The same 18-hole layout where a wounded Tiger battled his way to victory with a one-legged masterpiece at the 2008 U.S. Open.

Clay Hebert was the gracious friend who lent his "outside the bottle" perspective that day. Like an astute caddy standing behind a crouched player on the putting green, Clay read the break perfectly and saw with unblinking clarity what I could not. Huddled over lunch at a nearby taco stand, Clay said, "Watching you speak, it became abundantly clear... more than anything, you're a brand historian."

The puzzles pieces soon started falling together, including the August 2014 visit to the Louvre, when Dana and I watched a curious mob of spectators react to Da Vinci's

Mona Lisa. From there, the thesis quickly took shape, driven at the start by years of first-hand experiences shared with Jim and Dawna Gilbert and their used car dealership in Fredericton, New Brunswick. Jim and Dawna are the real heroes of this book: they are the people most responsible for showing us all—from any town or business category—what can happen when you believe in your own story. I will never be able to thank them enough for the gift of their friendship or applaud them enough for their courage.

The counterintuitive thinking that drove this book also originates from a long association with and personal admiration for what Roy H. Williams and his wife Pennie created with Wizard Academy in the heart of Texas. I first read *Secret Formulas of the Wizard of Ads* in March of 2000 while on a six-hour hockey road trip between Moncton, New Brunswick, and Cape Breton, Nova Scotia. After completing the trilogy and subscribing to Roy's weekly "Monday Morning Memo," I have since made about a dozen trips to the campus for a number of in-person classes and have recommended the experience to hundreds of others.

Many thanks to the husband-and-wife team of Joe and Justine Medeiros, the world's acknowledged experts and leading authorities on the greatest art theft in history. Their astonishing, award-winning documentary, *Mona Lisa Is Missing*, is a legend in its own right, beginning with Joe reading one line in a book about Leonardo Da Vinci that ignited an insatiable curiosity to discover the truth. Joe and Justine followed a twisted road that led through France and Italy and included connecting with the daughter of the thief, Celestina Peruggia. With factual and primary source documents, Joe and Justine have gained the respect of art historians and criminologists who can attest to their expertise on the subject, and I am grateful they took time to share those insights. You can learn more at monalisamissing.com.

The stories about Webers on Highway 11, Pike Place Fish Market and Café du Monde that anchor the second quarter of the book were inspired by what Roy shared at an August 2007 class and first reported in a MMMemo from October 31, 2005. Since that memo arrived on my 43rd birthday, I will consider it a perfectly symbolic way to communicate the many gifts that await should you ever enroll at Wizard Academy. Everyone owes it to themselves to make that journey to Austin at least once in their lifetime. I will forever consider myself a humble and grateful student and these pages are not long enough for me to express the appreciation I feel and the debt I owe for what Roy and Pennie have done for the world. Wizard Academy is also where I met my Texas Amigo, Ray Seggern, in April 2006. Besides developing the "Huggable" concept for Jim and Dawna, Ray has ZZ Top mojo to go with a heart bigger than all of Texas, and I am lucky to have a friend like him. Special thanks to Wizard of Ads partner Jeff Sexton of Pensacola, Florida, for his spectacular virtual writing class in January 2021, as well as to Daniel Whittington and the unforgettable Tour of Scotland at the Toad & Ostrich pub that makes every Wizard Academy experience something that must be tasted and savored.

Multiple visits to Webers on Highway 11, the Pike Place Fish Market and Café du Monde were also supported with multiple interviews and conversations. Tom Rennie was gracious enough to be interviewed for our *Leaders &*

Legends series and Mike McParland (a.k.a. "The Key Man") is a walking encyclopedia of information who was always happy to help. In April 2016, conversations with various fishmongers at the Seattle market helped fill in some of the blanks, but in New Orleans no one has any real answers or proof of what made Café du Monde iconic in the first place. Chic Miller from Toastmasters helped flesh out some of the mystery, but much of that story only exists in oral traditions. Say what you want, but when you are dealing with the spirit world and the occult powers of Madame Marie Laveau, perhaps it's a good idea to leave well enough alone.

Observations about Dollar Shave Club and former improv actor Michael Dubin came from hundreds of articles in publications such as *Inc.*, *Fortune*, *Forbes* and many others, as well as from watching Michael share his story in multiple YouTube videos. It helped that a friend of mine from Cincinnati who once served as a senior marketing chief at Procter & Gamble filled in some of the backstory of the business earthquakes caused by DSC. Out of respect for my friend, his or her name will not be disclosed and will be protected as vigorously as Colonel Sanders would safeguard his secret recipe of 11 herbs and spices.

The story of Nike and Bill Bowerman was inspired in part by a personal visit in October 2018 with Mr. Don Murray of Eugene, Oregon. Don was one of the original management consultants Phil Knight worked with to grow his company from the millions to the billions in revenues. Knight commissioned Don to write a book for 2,000 Nike insiders, a book that has not been released to the public but that allowed me to piece together the brand philosophy behind

SOURCES & ACKNOWLEDGMENTS

the "swoosh." Despite battling health issues, Don was in great spirits that day as he recounted his personal insights and memories. Sadly, Don passed away on June 1, 2021, but I hope he and members of his family know how much I cherish the memory of that visit. Other elements of the Nike story were shaped by Knight's 2016 memoir *Shoe Dog* as well as by Scott Bedbury's 2002 classic, *A New Brand World*. Scott, former head of marketing at Nike, also appeared on the *Not Real Art* podcast on February 9, 2021, with Scott "Sourdough" Power, and it was interesting to see how many of his insights not only stood the test of time, but also align with many of the principles outlined in this book.

Many thanks also to Jesse Cole of the Savannah Bananas, who shared his "Yellow Tux" approach to business and branding on a YouTube segment we uploaded April 27, 2020. When the global pandemic was at its height in terms of economic uncertainty, Jesse's leadership abilities and unwavering faith in how you build a legendary brand is still there for all to see. In much the same manner, Tim McClure of "Don't Mess With Texas" fame helped inspire the thinking that drove Chapter 7—long before we actually got to meet in person. He is known far and wide as the "John Wayne of Words," and you can see some of what the Duke and I talked about in a *Leaders & Legends* segment we posted on March 17, 2021. Thanks to platforms like LinkedIn and Zoom, Tim and I were able to connect, compare notes and seriously jawbone from decades of shared experiences on the power of Tribal Narratives—or what he refers to as a battle cry. Rest assured, Tim and I are kicking the dust around many ideas to create future brand legends and advance the noble and heroic cause of business mythmaking. Special thanks also to award-winning journalist, author and truth seeker A'Lelia Bundles for her insights on the story of her great-great grandmother. A'Lelia's keen eye for historical accuracy and a true reflection of the Madam C.J. Walker legacy was incredibly invaluable.

From a scientific perspective, conversations with Dr. Paul Zak and Dr. Polly Wiessner through 2019 and 2021 were instrumental in shaping ideas that support the neurological case for storytelling. Even though they come at the subject from very different backgrounds and perspectives, their conclusions are identical. During our research, there were countless other studies and experts that shared similar insights, but in the spirit of limiting intellectual overkill and page count, Dana and I decided that Paul and Polly offered plenty to go on, and I am thankful for their insight.

Any author will tell you that being able to see further ahead only happens when you stand on the shoulders of giants. Sir Isaac Newton first used that phrase in 1675 and it's still the perfect metaphor to explain the appreciation you have for those who came before you to pave new highways of intellectual progress. Seth Godin's 2003 classic *Purple Cow*, Christopher Booker's 800-page 2004 tome *The Seven Basic Plots* and Simon Sinek's 2019 observations from *The Infinite Game* are just a few of the selections from my personal library that helped clarify some fuzzy thoughts and sharpen rough edges on what's involved in creating a legendary brand. I would be remiss, however, if I did not give credit to Watty Piper's *The Little Engine That Could*. My late mother introduced me to that way of thinking as a three-year-old. It was the greatest gift she could have given to her only son. I can still hear her saying, "There's no such word as can't."

I first read Barb Stegemann's *7 Virtues of a Philosopher Queen* when a mutual friend mailed me a copy back in 2008. Her commitment to social justice and compassionate capitalism is one I have deeply admired for over a decade. A fellow East Coaster, Barb is one who truly lives her own brand. The parallels between her story and that of Madam C.J. Walker from a century ago also happened to align with what Rachel Mielke experienced starting her small business out on the prairies. Rachel appeared on the TEC Canada *Leadership Standard* podcast on June 15, 2020, and graciously took time on a number of subsequent phone calls to add sparkling color and detail to her experiences with the British monarchy. Coincidentally, on that same June 15 day, Captain Trevor Greene's TEDx Talk with Dr. Ryan D'Arcy was uploaded to YouTube. The research and writing of this book is filled with dozens of such coincidences.

My father having been born a decade apart to the September 10 birthday of Arnold Palmer was another such coincidence—as was Palmer being a licensed pilot with 20,000 flying hours, similar to Moose Jaw Mayor Fraser Tolmie, the only son of Scottish immigrants who earned his wings with the RCAF and who has also enjoyed a few rounds at The Old Course and several pints at the Dunvegan. My information on the legend of St Andrews stems from humbling rounds during back-to-back visits in 2016 and 2017. Huge thanks to John Boyne of Caddie Golf Tours for patiently showing me around the fabled links and imparting his love of Scotland and the crazy, endlessly maddening and wonderfully splendid game it gave the world.

Dad's personal scrapbook, filled with hundreds of newspaper articles from the '50s, '60s, '70s and '80s, was like a walk through a personal history I wish I had appreciated more while growing up. Our annual four-generational foursome with my son Ryan and grandson Cayden has been a wonderful way to rekindle some of the memories that helped make Chapter 12 come to light. Ryan and my sister, Karen Maxwell, also pull out all the stops to make sure our annual tournament has the proper MGA Invitational swag for all participants.

Research on the Gold & Silver in Las Vegas, Nevada, and Lambeau Field in Green Bay, Wisconsin, resulted from multiple personal visits to both locations from March of 2015 to February of 2020. You can learn a lot about consumer behavior by just browsing and eavesdropping: observing humans and how they respond to symbols and rituals when they don't know they're being studied. Touring the Green Bay Packers Hall of Fame in October 2018 with Jim Gilbert was a real eye-opener!

As an official, carded member of the Tennessee Squires Association, I have access to its private Facebook group, where postings revealed enormous insight on the extraordinary love affair that ordinary people have with brands and the stories they represent. Rick Harrison's memoir *License to Pawn* was a valuable source as Chapter 3 detailed the hiccups and highlights on the way to landing the gig on History Television. Page 251 of the 2011 Hyperion first edition of his book was especially insightful for the expletive-loaded admonishment from Harrison's father that the idea of pursuing a television show was pure nonsense. Bob Harlan's 2007 book *Green and Golden Moments* helped provide details of what was involved in the campaign to refurbish Lambeau Field. As a Lombardi fan since Jerry Kramer's *Instant Replay*, published in 1968, helped add layers to the Packers mythology, along with several other books, including 2009's *That First Season* by John Eisenberg and 1999's *When Pride Still Mattered* from David Maraniss. The intersection of Jack Daniel's, the Green Bay Packers and *Pawn Stars* was chosen as a set of parallel yet diverse examples that illustrate brand-building principles that can apply to any individual or organization.

The notoriety around the City of Moose Jaw was helped in no small part by TEC Canada chair and Rear Admiral of the Royal Saskatchewan Navy Paul Martin. It was Paul who put the bug in my ear about a pair of dads from Regina, Justin Reves and Greg Moore, who had gone viral with videos about the NHL's Vegas Golden Knights. It wasn't long before a friendship ensued and the duo catapulted the Moose Jaw brand with their hilarious exposé of the "Mac the Moose" scandal.

Justin and Greg deserve many thanks and accolades for being willing to battle harsh winter elements on January 11 to shoot and edit the video that became a social media broadside across Norway's bow. City of Moose Jaw communications director Craig Hemingway also stepped up to the plate numerous times to breathe poetic fuel into the story fire that supports the growing and global fascination with "Canada's Most Notorious City."

The concept of becoming your own media company stems from a Gary Vaynerchuk speech at the inaugural Archangel Summit in Toronto, Ontario, on September 21, 2016. His assertions that day helped crystalize what I had been feeling and noticing ever since we launched our own YouTube channel in July 2015. David Meerman Scott and Robert Rose were very helpful with what they graciously shared in several conversations about their books, including 2020's *Fanocracy* and *Killing Marketing* from 2017. I had been aware of the value of online video since 2008, when Jim Gilbert and I launched a series called CHCD-TV, but it wasn't until 17-year-old Josh Parlee showed me Casey Neistat's "Make It Count" video in 2015 that the vision for the future became abundantly clear.

Few people have played such a key role in my evolution as a writer and storyteller as Josh has. When he left university life at 19 to venture out as the owner of his own video production company, I knew there was a lot to learn by simply watching the world through his magically creative eyes. Besides being supremely talented, Josh has a no-limits, burn-the-midnight-oil work ethic. His tireless dedication to an evolving craft and small business makes me feel incredibly grateful to have had a front-row seat from Day One. His parents and family have every reason to be peacock proud of a gifted young man whose talents are only exceeded by his genuine humility and kindness.

A project of this magnitude does not happen without a small army of friends, supporters and idea generators who contributed mightily with advice, feedback and personal experiences. Bob Parker of The Pit Crew Challenge was an "outside the bottle" beast from beginning to end of several versions of the manuscript. Everyone should be so lucky as to have a friend and collaborator like Bob. From the same ballpark is my friend and #1 mensch Jamie Mason Cohen, founder of a creative problem-solving program called Saturday Night Leaders. Another fellow author and professional speaker, Jamie is like that great left-hander you can count on in the late innings to come out of the bullpen, uncork a troubleshooting split-fingered fastball and save whatever project you're working on.

I am truly blessed to have such gracious and insightful sounding boards like Bob and Jamie, who spent dozens of hours listening to half-baked ideas when they were still in a fragile, embryonic state.

The best kind of friends are the ones who can see right through us and still enjoy the view. A former television co-host from our days with *Sports Monday*, Allan Power is also that rare friend who challenges you to be your best without any lecturing or sermonizing. A former NHL scout with Chicago and Toronto, Allan possesses an incredible fountain of wisdom that I feel privileged to drink from. Likewise, accountant Denis Goguen has been an ally from the start—every entrepreneur can benefit when you have a guy like Denis on your side. Many other friends also contributed greatly with their feedback and, at the risk of omitting anyone, many thanks to Bob Lennon, Tim Beach, Lisa "Longball" Vlooswyk, Andrew Oland, Matthew Oland, Bryan Eisenberg, Dan Martell, Martin Latulippe, Don Schmincke, Ruth-Anne Marley, "Antarctic" Mike Pierce, Sandy Gillis, Darrin Mitchell, "Smokin'" Joe Howard, Kimberly King,

Leo Bottary, "The Okanagan Kid" Rod Anderson and "Virtuoso of Vision" Ken MacLeod.

Many thanks to early believers from TEC Canada and Vistage International, including group chairs Mike Mallory, André Turcotte, Tony Schy, Dave Weinkauf, "Pub Crawler" Andy Marsh from the U.K., Lonnie Martin, Tom Foster, Julia Oulton, John Howman, David MacLean, Shaune Eldred, Marty Stowe and "Emperor of Ottawa" Pascal St-Jean. If the greatest gift of life is friendship, I have been blessed to have received it many times over.

It's also why I consider myself fortunate to work with publishing visionary Jesse Finkelstein and the top-notch crew of professionals at Page Two. In my completely and thoroughly biased view, Jesse and her partner Trena White have emerged as the Big Little Legends of the modern-day publishing industry. There are so many people at Page Two to thank, including Caela Moffet, Rony Ganon, Amanda Lewis, Peter Cocking, Jennifer Lum and Chris Brandt, who all helped keep this project on the straight and narrow. If writing this book was like driving a car, it was a joy to have development editor Melissa Edwards ride shotgun and keep us between the mustard and the mayonnaise on the long way home.

Like any lengthy road trip, the process of writing a book begins long before the actual journey: in this case, it started even before Clay Hebert and I got together at Torrey Pines in 2018. Truth be told, this odyssey began when Dana Zilic introduced me to Paulo Coelho and *The Alchemist* in 2009.

Life has never been the same since.

On both a personal and professional level, Dana has been there every step of the way. Heavily armed with her own brand of curiosity, she has stepped forward to dig through more than 30 scientific and medical research papers that explore the undeniable links to the timeless power of storytelling. No matter how much she tries to shrug it off, her fingerprints are all over this book and to this day I still see her as a global authority on Coelho's masterpiece. There have been many great partnerships over the years in business and life—Bogart and Bacall, Lennon and McCartney, Jagger and Richards, Jobs and Wozniak—but I'll stack ours up against anyone. Dana is the rock to my roll, the pearl to my oyster shell and the one person most responsible for making this concept of *Big Little Legends* become a reality. It hasn't always been sunshine, rainbows and lollipops. Like any couple who share life, kids, three dogs and a growing business, we've experienced our share of ups, downs, grits and porkchops. Together, we have weathered our inevitable share of storms and fought what has felt like losing battles. In many ways, she is the real-life description of how Love is described in Corinthians 13:4: "Love is patient, love is kind. It does not envy, it does not boast, it is not proud. It always protects, always trusts, always hopes, always perseveres." Like that private motivational speech she belted out over the phone at a Crunch Time Moment prior to a 2012 conference with the Apple Specialist Marketing Group in Minneapolis! Through Dana, I have learned that sharing the foxhole of life with someone you can truly count on and trust is the only thing that matters. In the end, all we have is each other, the home front we share with our furry, four-legged friends Theodore, Sophie and Maggie, and the legacy we create for our families and those we care deeply about.

That's why the incredibly heroic Tiger Woods story from the 2008 U.S. Open is a perfect metaphor for any one of us who has struggled with anguish and agony. Returning to action just two months after arthroscopic knee surgery, the stiff, rusty and still aching Woods hobbled and grimaced with every shot as he pushed through the searing pain to win his 14th major title. Over four riveting rounds and a grueling 19-hole playoff, Woods didn't finesse the golf course. He attacked it like a back-alley streetfighter. At times, his bad leg would buckle under the pressure of a swing. His twisted, contorted face told the entire story of the son of a Green Beret, determined to soldier on. When the final putt finally dropped on that historic June afternoon in La Jolla, Tiger Woods demonstrated an essential quality of all legends: a stubborn refusal to give up or give in and the decision that failure is not an option.

It is my hope that *Big Little Legends* emulates and reflects some of the finer qualities revealed by any gutsy and courageous performance, like the ones I have witnessed privately with my own father and with Dana Zilic. From completely different backgrounds, they are my personal heroes for demonstrating unbreakable will and unrelenting focus. In much the same manner, this book may not be pretty at times, but the intention is to arouse an inner desire to discover your inner Tiger and embark on a hunt to build modern-day legacy.

Legends are never content to play it safe.

They don't follow the same rules as everybody else.

You don't have to either.

*You have to look at the past
in order to learn from it and move on.*

TIGER WOODS

ABOUT THE AUTHOR

GAIR MAXWELL is a storyteller, brand strategist and self-described history junkie who marvels at the sight and sound of a well-struck drive off the tee. A frequent-flying keynote speaker, he has shared speaking stages with icons such as Richard Branson and Gene Simmons, and was named Speaker of the Year by TEC Canada, the country's largest CEO organization.

Gair is an accredited Tennessee Squire, preferring Jack Daniel's on the rocks and a cold Moosehead. A life-long fan of Van Halen, he believes both versions of the band—the one with David Lee Roth and the one with Sammy Hagar—should be considered legendary. Gair currently resides in London, Ontario, with his business and life partner, Dana Zilic, and their brood of two cocker spaniels (Theodore & Sophie) and a beagle-mix rescue named Maggie. *Big Little Legends* is his second book.

gairmaxwell.com